THE SALES PROFESSIONAL'S LIBRARY

This new series is designed for all sales people who are determined to get to the top of their profession. Whether you're new to selling or looking to accelerate your career, the titles in this series will help you:

- Improve your selling skills
- Understand sales and marketing techniques
- Increase your knowledge and expertise
- Boost your self-confidence and career prospects.

Every title is:

- Packed with sensible advice
- Full of action guidelines
- Refreshingly free of gimmicks and jargon
- Written by experts.

The first three titles available are:

First Division Selling
One Foot on the Management Ladder
Prospecting for Customers

Forthcoming titles are:

Successful Large Account Management
How to Overcome Objections
The Art of Telephone Selling
How to Speak with Conviction

To find out more about *The Sales Professional's Library*, please contact:

Kogan Page, 120 Pentonville Road, London N1 9JN
Tel: 071-278 0433 Fax: 071-837 6348

FIRST DIVISION SELLING

ROBERT VICAR

KOGAN
PAGE

First published in 1991 as *One Foot in the Door*, by Buckley Press Ltd, 58 Fleet Street, London EC4Y 1JA.

This edition published by Kogan Page in 1993.

Kogan Page Limited
120 Pentonville Road
London N1 9JN

British Library Cataloguing in Publication Data

A CIP record for this book is available from the British Library.

ISBN 0 7494 1191 0

Typeset by Books Unlimited (Nottm), Sutton-in-Ashfield, NG17 1AL

Printed in England by Clays Ltd, St Ives plc

Preface

As a child, my first experience of a salesman came with the reading of Red Riding Hood when the *Kleeneeze*-equipped wolf arrived at grandmother's door to persuade her to allow him to enter. It would be difficult to imagine a more unlikely sales success story, faced, as the wolf was, with all the disadvantages that he carried with him.

Even if we forget the fact that his prospect was a somewhat senile pensioner, the wolf had, nevertheless, to persuade her that he, the salesman, was a man to be trusted, that he had a product that she required, and that she should be prepared to let him through the door to discuss his wares.

With this book at his elbow, he might well have found the whole job easier, even though, on the face of it, the eating of grandmother and the subsequent seduction of Red Riding Hood would seem success enough. However you might, on reflection, think that life in the selling game is not really like that and, in the real world, the wolf would have been unlikely even to have made first base.

This book outlines the techniques which will improve your *own* sales skills and teaches you the discipline of using your selling time more effectively. It will take you through the basic principles that you should use and will guide you on using and developing the talents that you probably already have.

Robert Vicar
1993

Acknowledgements

Acknowledgement must be made to all those, both famous and also less well known, whose apt words have occasionally been quoted in the text and chapter headings of this book. My only wish is that I had thought of them first myself. Many of the quotations have been taken from various anthologies and I should like to acknowledge the assistance of the compilers of the following collections whose work made the finding of appropriate quotations somewhat easier:

The Bloomsbury Thematic Dictionary of Quotations compiled by the Bloomsbury Publishing Co., London W1V 5DE

A Treasury of Business Quotations compiled by Michael C Thomsett and published by St James Press, London W1P 9FA

The Speakers Handbook of Epigrams and Witticisms compiled by Herbert V Prochnow and published by A Thomas and Co. Ltd, Blackpool, Lancashire

The Speakers Digest of Quotations compiled by Rolfe White and published by W Foulsham and Co Ltd, Yeovil Road, Slough, Berkshire

Chambers Book of Quotations compiled by Robert I Fitzhenry and published by W and R Chambers Ltd, 43–45 Annadale Street, Edinburgh, EH7 4AZ

Bartletts Unfamiliar Quotations compiled by Leonard Louis Levinson, and published by Unwin Hyman Ltd, 15–17 Broadwick Street, London, W1V 1FP

Acknowledgement is made to Winston Fletcher for the quotation from his book *Super Efficiency* used in Chapter Four.

Acknowledgement is made to John Fenton for the quotation from his book *How to sell against competition* used in Chapter Nine.

Also my acknowledgements as follows:

To Groucho Marx quoted in Chapter Two.

To Maxell Haltz quoted in Chapter Three.

To Ralph Bunch quoted in Chapter Four.

To Stephen Leacock quoted in Chapter Five.

To Marty Allen quoted in Chapter Eight.

To Ben Feldman quoted in Chapter Nine.

To Elizabeth Bowen quoted in Chapter Nine.

To Troy Gordon quoted in Chapter Eleven.

To Channing Pollock quoted in Chapter Fifteen.

To Gellett Burgess quoted in Chapter Fifteen.

Robert Vicar 1993

We are all involved in selling

‘*A man without a smiling face must not open a shop*’
Chinese Proverb

THE SALES ETHIC AND CONSUMER CHOICE

Anyone who deals with customers is in the selling business. Whether that person is a doctor or a bricklayer, a service is being offered and whilst the methods that are used may differ, a free public that has a choice must be persuaded to use that service. If the supplier is a monopoly, there will be less incentive to please the final user, who, in the last analysis, has nowhere else to go, but real monopolies are rare indeed. In fact, if one were to take out the Prison Service, the Income Tax Office and the DSS, we would be hard pushed to find any organisation which would not be totally lost without a final market for its product. If gas is too expensive we will use electricity, if trains are too costly we will use coaches, and if the telephone rates become excessive, we will not use the system at all. Whatever we supply, whether it is insurance or battleships, we live and breathe by our ability to convince our customers that we have a better service or product than that of our competitors.

As Robert Louis Stevenson said, 'Everyone lives by selling something'. The theory operates even in our private lives where, for all our ideas on discipline and control, both parents and teachers need to sell themselves to the children in their care in order to secure the children's respect and agreement for the standards they are being taught. There is no one who is not, in some way, a salesman, and there will be few who cannot benefit in their chosen professions by knowing and operating the basic rules of selling.

In business basics, selling is the sharp end of marketing. It is the final element in a process that began with a decision that a particular market was right for a particular product and it relies totally on that original concept being a correct one. However, once the marketing decision *has* been made, and the product or service is available, it is the salesman, and the salesman *only*, who then carries the responsibility of finding the prospects and convincing them of the benefits of buying. Those who, in the past, believed that the quality of the product itself could find the customers, that the product 'spoke for itself', were those who eventually relinquished their market to their competitors.

A salesman must have many skills at his elbow, but in the end his sole job is to persuade his customers, firstly that they want to deal with him or his company, and secondly that the product or service he is offering represents as good, or better, value as the prospect is likely to get anywhere else. Different prospects may have different reasons for buying the same product, and it is the prime job of the salesman to analyse that reason, but essentially they will all buy because of the confidence they have in the product and the man selling it. They will only buy solely on price if all else is equal; it is the job of the salesman to ensure that all the other factors are *not* equal.

We have, in the past few decades, seen a revolution in the way sales professionals are regarded. From that era when companies were run by accountants, we now see many more operations run by larger than life sales entrepreneurs. Even the cost-conscious accountants have come to realise that without effective sales professionals at the end of the line to move the product into the market, there is little point in manufacturing it in the first place. There will always be unprofessional and ineffective salesmen but in the harsher markets of Europe where we will have to earn our living in the future, we will have to compete more and more with European companies who, historically, have always given to the sales profession the importance that it deserves.

You may well have a regular training programme in your company, but if such a programme is not available, it will be even more important for you to develop sales skills on your own. There is no way that those skills will just happen, either by chance or even as a result of long experience unless you guide them in the way that they should go. What is more likely to happen is that bad selling habits will become part of your presentation without your even being aware of them. Unfortunately, without a critical sales manager at your elbow, you will rarely find out about your own errors except eventually from your falling sales figures, and perhaps not even then. Self criticism, if the other kind is not available, is the hard way of learning, but do it you must and at least you have started by buying (or being given) this book. If you at least *know* what you should be doing, you have a chance of determining whether you are actually following a recommended course or not.

Selling, for all the popular misconceptions, has never been a question of being affable and generally well-liked. Certainly that helps, but unless you have also developed yourself to operate in a certain way, you will merely become the well-liked loser.

Selling, in the form of bartering, is a part of our daily lives. Husbands sell to their wives and vice versa, but most of this is simply doing what our natural instinct tells us is the best way to secure what we want. If you wish, you too can leave everything to chance and even, by the law of averages, be moderately successful, but it is surely more sensible to leave less to chance and make the whole job easier by finding a framework in which to work. The illogical fact is that there are very few salespeople who could not tell you what that general framework is, but a good five out of every ten will admit that in their everyday selling, they simply do not use it as they should. It is really not difficult to take the step which makes your selling success both more consistent, and, in the long run, more pleasurable, but in the end, all the suggestions and rules in this book will be of little value if they are not consciously put into practice. After all, every other profession works to a pattern and uses a rigid method of working to achieve what is necessary. As sales professionals, we demean ourselves if we think that our own methods of working can be approached any differently, or that the training for it should be regarded any less seriously.

In our world there are still some who will claim that if a product stands head and shoulders above the rest, then it will, through quality alone, find its rightful share of the available market. But history shows that the road to financial ruin is well worn by those who managed to produce a product that people both wanted and needed but who then either failed to tell the world what was on offer, or dealt inadequately with the customers that they *did* manage to contact. It is also certainly true that many inferior products, some overpriced, make their way in the market through hard selling and by sales techniques which are better than those of their competitors.

Your business, whether large or small, is no exception to these rules. I hope that those of you who read this manual who are not directly salesmen or saleswomen, will come to realise that the selling job is a great deal more than the company car and the Friday walk round the golf course (if anyone indeed is that lucky!).

However, those of you who are already in the sales profession may need to be reminded that out in the world there are many others like yourself who will be offering a competitively priced product similar to your own. Those competitive salespeople will also be well-dressed, polite and articulate and will have spent time in learning how best to turn the customers their way. To succeed, you will need to do it better and more professionally than they do. There is no way you are going to do that without a great deal of hard work and persistence. Follow the guidance in this manual and you will not only be pointing in the right direction but you will also have at your elbow a set of cast-iron rules to refer to on those occasions when things seem to be going wrong.

THE BASIC ATTRIBUTES

The equipment of any salesman must inevitably include an effective and usable working knowledge of the product or service that he sells, a skill of assessment which enables him to analyse and sort out those who might want that service and also an ability to decide when they are ready to do business with him. He must then develop the art of persuasion to a level where he can convey that knowledge to his prospective customer and develop also the personality, enthusiasm and determination which will be the hallmark of his style and which will get him orders. Some of the attributes he may already have. Many will have to be learnt and the sales professional who already believes he has them all probably needs this book more than most.

Most errors in selling are made, not because we are unaware of what should be done, but because we fail to put into practice the rules which we know by experience will secure more sales. As with any other skill, selling is a discipline which will work for you if you persist at it and rely on its principles. Selling by luck alone is hard, unnecessary, and generally unsuccessful.

CHECKLIST

■ Effective persuasion is part of all our lives.

■ Professionalism in selling does not just happen on its own.

■ Don't become the well-liked loser.

■ Your competitors will also be professionals.

■ Product knowledge is essential.

■ Customer knowledge is equally vital.

2

The first impression

'I never forget a face, but I'll make an exception in your case.'
Groucho Marx

THE FIRST HURDLE—PUBLIC SUSPICION

There is a widely held view that salesmen, unlike all other people in the workplace, are somehow born with their selling talents, and that whilst they may be able to sharpen those talents, their skills are based far more on natural ability than on training and development.

If that were so, there would be little point in your reading this manual and less point in my writing it. I would even go as far as to say that the publicly held belief of what makes a good salesman is responsible for more bad salesmanship than almost anything else, and certainly has played its part in creating the bad image that the sales profession sometimes projects.

In many people's minds, the picture of the conventional salesman is that of a fast talking operator who is somehow smarter than the people to whom he is selling and who is a success because of that talent. Television programmes featuring the likes of Arthur Daley or Del Boy do little to improve that image and the American electioneering slogan of 'Would you buy a second hand car from this man?' indicates that public suspicion of the job that you are doing is probably your first obstacle. If you do not believe me, think of the many variations of job title which have been invented to avoid calling you what you are – a salesman. You may well be called a sales engineer, a marketing executive, an investment consultant, even the vague title of company representative, but your job is to sell and if you do not do that, you are of little use to the company that employs you.

FIRST IMPRESSIONS ARE VITAL

So, having identified your first obstacle, let us look at the best way of overcoming it. You have not yet met up with your client, he knows nothing about you, and the *first impression* that you create will be all important. Indeed, if you fail to secure that favourable first impression, life becomes immediately difficult.

At some time we will all have witnessed a person entering a shop to register what may very well be a valid complaint, and while explaining his complaint that person then starts to raise his voice to shout at the assistant or the manager. Unbelievably, the customer, who is looking for his problem to be resolved, goes out of his way to alienate the one person who can solve it. The opportunity to make an immediately favourable impression has been lost and cannot be recovered. Remember that even someone making a complaint has a selling job to do in order to achieve what he wants.

I would not suggest that in your own selling you are consciously alienating your customers, but let us see whether you can improve that initial moment when you face your customer for the first time. The advice that is given, both in this chapter and in the remainder of the book, will apply whether you are calling on large international companies offering major equipment or services, or whether you are making calls on the man at home who is looking at double glazing or possibly his first life policy. There is really no difference in the approach that should be made, except possibly that in the latter case, you are more likely to be able to secure a swift decision from the one decision maker with whom you are dealing.

WORK AT THE FIRST IMPRESSION

It is vital that you get your first introduction right. Whenever that initial contact is made with a customer, there will be a reaction or response. You may well have boosted your own or your company image, you may even have damaged it or you may have made no impact at all. This will all happen in the initial moment of meeting and will decide whether you are going to get the chance to go any further and will govern how hard or easy it is going to be to secure the business when you *do* ask for it. Many people will tell you that the sale is often made in the first moment of your call. It is worthwhile remembering that many sales are probably lost in that first moment also.

We are all aware of the poor impression given by a weak handshake. The customer can get away with it – you can't. Your handshake will, in many instances, be your first real contact with your customer, and he will be as keen as you to analyse the kind of person that he is dealing with. So, having got that right, what about the rest of your image?

The state of your company car could well be taken as a mirror of your own attitude to life, and your arrival in anything other than an immaculate vehicle can only be to your disadvantage. The way that you dress is obviously important and you would be foolish, or else an extremely good salesman, to think that you can buck the system and still be successful. It is here that the 'empathy' approach becomes important so that your buyer accepts you as someone with whom he can identify.

DRESS FOR THE OCCASION

Depending on what product you are selling or promoting, you will need to decide how to dress to meet that situation. It is equally wrong to sell finance dressed too casually as it is to sell plant hire dressed too elegantly. Go into a City office in Bermuda shorts if you wish. You will certainly get a good laugh and probably also ensure that you are never forgotten, but I would question whether you will get any business. Indeed, anything about your dress or your appearance which distracts your prospect must be wrong and whilst those distractions may not make business impossible, they will certainly make it more difficult.

Make it your ideal not to look less (or more) affluent than your customer, and, regardless of the industry in which you are working, you must always work hard to look as if you belong to that particular environment. Remember that you do not always have to dress neatly and tidily, although generally it helps, but you *must* always dress to match the occasion. There are, of course, situations where the customer will expect you to project an image which gives him confidence in dealing with you, and it will be your skill in balancing this against looking out of place, that will achieve the result of meeting his expectations.

Having looked at and improved your appearance to the best of your ability, your next problem will be the actual impression that you create when you arrive on your customer's doorstep. Many years ago, I worked alongside a sales manager who knew well how effective those first moments could be. As he entered his customer's office, he was carrying his document case, wearing his overcoat, and carrying his hat, the latter being part of every salesman's uniform at the time. He always took off his coat, found a hook on which to hang it, did the same with his hat and then lodged his document case on the desk in front of him. Without saying it, and before he had even commenced his sales opening, he had established that he had something important to say and was likely to be in that office until he had said it. He had created an environment where he expected to be regarded seriously. Can we all say with conviction that we set the scene in the same sort of way?

A word of caution, however: always ask permission before you use your prospect's office or home as your own. Ask before you hang up your coat, wait until he suggests it before you sit down in what may be his favourite chair. Before you use his desk or table as a demonstration area – ask. All these actions will show you as courteous and professional and that you are prepared to make an effort in your presentation to the client. Believe me, he will notice. And lastly, *do not smoke*. It used to be acceptable: it isn't now.

OTHER PEOPLE CAN HELP

While you must always be looking at ways to improve your image, it is necessary to remember that the first impression may well be created not by ourselves but by a third party, such as a receptionist or secretary whose job it is to filter the number of people who want to get through the door to meet her boss. You will usually not even be present when the secretary says to the person you want to see, 'That infuriating Mr Hamshawe is here again, shall I tell him to see Mr Spriggs?' and, as you go out, you will never know why you do not reach first base.

How much better if the secretary were to say, 'That nice Mr Hamshawe is in reception and would like to see you. He assures me that he will not take much of your time. Can you spare five minutes?' I hardly have to tell you which approach is more likely to secure your interview. You will, however, only get that kind of assistance if you work on it and the sales professional who takes the trouble to comment that the secretary is 'looking smart today'; 'has a new hair style'; and 'how was the holiday in Ibiza?' will find that interest of this kind will generate a friendship and cooperation which will be of incalculable help when you call at that office in the future.

But, and this is a very important but, ensure that the personal information on your customer and his colleagues is correct, and also that you are able to remember it the next time that you call. If your memory is bad, then record the information that you have gleaned. It is better to use no Christian name than to use the wrong one and equally important to find out whether his Christian name should be used at all. It will, I hope, go without saying (almost), that every item of information which might be of use to you the next time you call must be recorded on whatever customer record card you or your company use. I just do not believe that there are people who can remember all the relevant facts without some kind of *aide-mémoire*, and I know how I react when someone who should know better addresses me by the wrong Christian name. Don't take the risk.

Finally, in all your relationships with the employees who you will meet on your way through to the man you will be selling to, always speak from a position of authority. The wrong kind of over-familiarity with any receptionist or secretary will eventually rebound on you. Remember that any employee of the company to which you are selling will have his or her main loyalties to those who are issuing the pay cheques. It is essential to establish yourself as a man who is on an equal footing with the Chief, not with the Indians.

You have now made your initial contacts and have done all you can to ensure that the first impression, over the telephone or whatever, is as persuasive as it can be. You are now in a position to talk to your client in person and you will need to make your point clearly, positively and effectively. In short, you will need to develop from a salesperson into a sales professional. How do you achieve it? Read on....

CHECKLIST

■ The salesperson — born or trained?

■ Your only job is to *sell*.

■ Get it right from the start.

■ Your appearance *does* matter.

■ Use others to help your cause.

■ Get all your facts straight — and *record* them.

■ Develop your authority so that it shows.

3

You must first sell yourself

'The most important sale in life is to sell yourself to yourself.'
Maxell Haltz

This selling yourself to your prospect is the next step forwards from the initial first impression that you have created, and, having taken all that trouble to build up the expectations of your customer, you must now live up to that reputation.

PUNCTUALITY: THE POLITENESS OF KINGS

First, and I am aware that this seems to be stating the obvious, if you have made an appointment for a specific time, *be there*. It was Louis XVIII who said that punctuality is the politeness of kings, but he also said that it was the duty of gentlemen and the necessity of men of business. Five minutes late *will* be noticed and equally thirty minutes early indicates that you cannot organise your own time efficiently.

If you arrive exactly at the moment that you said you would, your customer, who might even be regretting having given you an appointment in the first place, will find it difficult to fault you. Arrive early or late, and if he has any doubts about you or your product, you have given him the reason he needs to be negative in his reaction. In addition, if you start by showing that you mean what you say, your customer will find it much easier to believe you later when you offer a proposal which he also expects you to honour. Do this as a matter of course whenever you deal with your new business contacts and they will automatically assume that your negotiations with them will be conducted on the same reliable basis. Respecting the time of someone else is a common courtesy, but while as a seller you may feel that you also have a right to that respect, it would still be foolish to get too uptight when the seller doesn't have the same regard for your time.

It is also good advice to make your appointments, not on the hour or half hour but at specific times in between. Psychologically, the use of an exact hour or even half-hour implies that you are going to be there for at least 30 minutes, while a buyer or client who agrees to meet you at, say 3.10 pm. will be thinking that in twenty minutes time he can be free again. Obviously, the length of time you are actually there will depend on the impact you make when you get in front of him. But, and this is even more important when you select a specific time in this way, arrive exactly at the moment you said you would.

STICK TO YOUR PROMISES

In the same way, to maintain your reputation as someone who can be relied on, you must, during your discussions, make a firm note of all that you have been asked, or have promised to do, whether it is to send a confirming quotation, make an inquiry on your customer's behalf, or even to carry out some personal favour where you have offered to secure some information. When you are selling, there is no rule which says you have to offer any of these services but if you don't intend to fulfil a promise, or cannot remember to, it is far better not to make that promise in the first place. Remember that whatever you offer to do, you are putting your own reputation on the line and it is eventually the quality of that reputation which will secure you the order.

BUILD A RELATIONSHIP WITH YOUR CLIENT

To be successful in the selling profession, the simple rule is that you must aim to build a relationship with your client which will make him come to you rather than to your competitor. That competitor will also be a professional and will be equally competent in using his skills to reach the same target you are aiming for. Your only armour is to make sure that *you* are the man the customer most wants to deal with, and this advantage can, I assure you, make up for all sorts of areas where your product possibly falls short of what he is expecting of it. If, of course, your product also is a winner, then you have it made.

It should not be difficult in the very early stages of any meeting to find some common ground with your customer so that you create a situation where he is as interested in you as you are in him. Even on the occasions when your natural instincts tell you that it is the last thing you want to do, and is sometimes will be, you must *build a friendship with your customer*.

GET TO KNOW YOUR CUSTOMER

Leaving all else aside, it will certainly make the profession you have chosen more enjoyable, and while you cannot be expected to become close to everyone with whom you deal, nevertheless it is not difficult to get into the habit of telephoning your customers whenever you have that spare moment, showing interest in how their business is doing and what their prospects are for the future and, equally important, showing interest in other matters which may have arisen in a previous conversation. Get to know your customer personally both in his business and his social interests. Opportunities to get closer to your customer are arising all the time but the average salesman is really never wide awake enough to listen. Make sure you discover what interests him as otherwise it is unlikely you will ever succeed in arousing his own interest in you.

However, remember that while general social conversation can often ease the way to securing an eventual order, it will never actually get that order and must always be kept in perspective to the selling job that you are aiming to complete. Many salesmen tend to forget the essential rule of knowing *why* they are making a sales call, and the satisfaction of having had an enjoyable exchange of views about everything else, often clouds the problem that business was not discussed at all.

Never forget also that some buyers will actually prefer, until they know the salesperson extremely well, to separate their business life from their social life and can even consider too much interest in the second as an intrusion. Be warned that many will not tell you if you step over that dividing line, and that by doing so you are building a barrier against securing business in the future.

A buyer will always recognise a businesslike and detached approach for what it is, and will usually appreciate the respect you have for his time. You are not a social worker aiming to sort out the problems of your customer. Your sole job is to find out as swiftly as possible whether there is business to be secured and to decide whether you can secure it. That is what you are paid for.

If the product being sold is more or less equal to that sold by a competitor, people will normally buy from a friend whose company they enjoy, and whose integrity they know, rather than from a total stranger. Particularly if you are handling an inferior product (and someone has to), you can often use that friendship to secure an order against all the technical odds. There is only one alternative to dealing with friends and that is dealing with enemies, or at best customers who are neither one nor the other. If that is going to be the alternative you opt for, the service or product you are selling had better be the best available.

DEMONSTRATE A BREADTH OF KNOWLEDGE

While reliance on the goodwill of your customer and the acceptability of your own personality are both vital requirements, a further part of the image you project must necessarily be that of a man who knows what he is talking about. This does not just mean the ability to answer the technical queries that will be thrown at you because I would expect that to be part of your armoury as a matter of course. Ignorance of your product or of the services you have available will, without exception, irritate your prospect who will expect you to have all the answers. You must always know what you can offer, and know also how your company works and what decisions it can accept.

What is equally important is your own general knowledge, both of your customer's industry and the type of problem he is asking you to solve. If you are able also to quote the names of satisfied customers in the same industry who presented you with a similar problem and who, as a result of talking to you, satisfactorily solved that problem, then use their names to back your own authority. There is nothing as effective as an unbiased testimonial and if you can get your client to telephone those contacts, so much the better. You should, so long as you have ensured that the customer you recommend *is* happy with what he has got, gain immeasurably from the enthusiasm which your client will pass on to your new prospect. And, whilst we are at it, make sure that you cultivate your own enthusiasm about your product and your company. There is little hope in encouraging others to be enthusiastic if you cannot project that feeling yourself.

RELAX! BE YOURSELF!

When talking about how best to sell yourself to your customers, there is one rule above all others which, if you ignore it and go your own way, will bring you a life of frustration and guaranteed failure. That rule is simply – *relax and be yourself.* If, for example, you have convinced yourself that the only salesman who can survive is the loud-mouthed, beer-swilling extrovert, then unless you actually are one, you will have an impossible life projecting an image which does not come naturally to you. There is certainly no single formula for real sales success, nor is there ever a requirement to act a part in order to meet some false criteria which you have set. Obviously, if your personality is such that meeting people does not come easily to you, then you should seriously consider some other job than selling, for you can be assured that even the slowest witted of your customers will eventually sort you out and if they do not believe in *you* they will not believe in what you are selling either. You can always adjust your own presentation to match the wavelength of the man you are talking to but don't pretend to be the world's greatest yachtsman if you don't know a spinnaker from a rudder.

Remember that probably more sales are lost because the customer does not like the salesman or his company than are lost because the customer does not like the product. This is why good salesmen are paid good rewards to sell what are often indifferent or difficult products. If you don't believe me, check out the salaries and commission paid to successful timeshare salesmen promoting their wares in the Spanish holiday resorts.

CHECKLIST

- ■ Be punctual; that means neither early nor late.
- ■ Carry out the promises that you make.
- ■ Build a relationship with your client.
- ■ Know everything about your own product.
- ■ Know everything about your competitor's product.
- ■ Know the industry to which you are selling.
- ■ Don't play-act. Be yourself.

4

Face to face with your customer

'If you want to get across an idea, wrap it up in a person.'
Ralph Bunch

So, all being well, you now have the attention of the man who has the ability to give you his business. You have effectively sold yourself to him and now he is waiting to hear what you have to say about the product or service that you wish to offer. You should now launch into your sales presentation and convince him of what you are able to do for him or for his company. *Or should you?*

The answer to that question is certainly *no* and for many very good reasons. In the first place, there are very few people in this world who wouldn't rather be talking than listening and so far, the creation of your image being all important, you really haven't given him a chance. But far more important, what he has to say to you about himself and his needs for the future, and even the availability of his own or his company's finances, could alter the whole basis of the sales presentation you are just about to make.

GET YOUR CUSTOMER TALKING

I appreciate that you may well have done all the research you can regarding your client, but he will still have a great deal of additional information available which will be of assistance to you. You need to have that information and to do that you must get him talking. As I was told by my first sales manager over 35 years ago, 'Your two most valuable selling aids are fixed on either side of your head. Use them to listen to the customer. He will probably tell you what he is looking for without your even having to ask him.' Getting your customer talking is a great deal easier than you might think.

While you are listening, it is essential that from the beginning you look at the problem from the buyer's point of view. Particularly when you are dealing with large companies, you can fall into the trap of regarding the man facing you as a somewhat impersonal employee, acting only in the interests of his company and without emotions and viewpoints of his own. It is important that at an early stage those individual viewpoints are recognised so that you can take them into account when presenting your case. This does not necessarily mean that you must always agree with your customer's point of view, but it would be a very foolish salesman who did not know what that point of view was. If you do not have 'empathy', which simply means understanding the situation from the buyer's angle, you will always find it difficult to make your presentation acceptable to anyone other than yourself.

From my own experience, it is never too difficult to start your buyer talking about either himself or his business — in fact your problem may well be getting him to stop – but stop he certainly will if you fail to listen attentively, react to whatever he has to say, and contribute occasionally with your own comments to show your interest. After all, if he is going to buy from you, you are going to get involved in his affairs or business and he will want to know that your interest is genuine. Most of all, remember that what he is telling you can be used subsequently to good effect when you begin to persuade him how the product or service you are selling will benefit him in the business he has been discussing. If you fail to pay attention and do not take note of what you are being told about his business, you need not be surprised later when you cannot offer any advantages on how he might run that business better.

When you have asked all the questions you can, and listened to the replies, you should have a clear idea in your own mind what the customer is looking for, whether he has found it in the product or service he is currently using or is considering as an alternative to your own, and if not, some idea of whether your product or service could provide the answer. You should now, from the notes you will have taken during the meeting, summarise all the points you have discussed and check with him that what you have said accurately depicts the situation.

If you do this well, you will establish your own credibility and give the customer confidence that you have a good idea of what you are talking about. The main object of summarising in this way is to create a basis of agreed points on which you can fall back as you progress the sale. The aim is, of course, to lay down the detail where you both agree and at the same time create a situation where you do not have to go back over the same ground again. Then, should you find some stumbling block in your discussion at a later point, you do not have to go back right to the beginning but can restart your sales presentation at a point where your customer will again be agreeing with you.

THE IMPORTANCE OF LISTENING

As with your other sales techniques, listening is a discipline which requires to be learnt. To train yourself in the skill of listening effectively, a few simple guidelines will be of help:

- Give your total concentration to the person who is speaking and to what is being said. Most of us have a range of different problems on our minds at any one time, and it is essential to put them to one side, certainly until the conversation is over. A buyer will realise, probably before you do yourself, that he is no longer holding your interest.

- Aim to show your involvement by intermittently asking questions and responding to what has been said. Even when the replies to such questions are not of consequence, they are still vital if you are to secure the prospect's own confidence in you.

- Always be ready to listen to the *whole* problem before you offer a solution or a proposal. This, more than anything else, will discipline your listening so that, if your customer already has a firm opinion of his own, you do not unwittingly present suggestions which are in strong contradiction to his own views.

- Be constantly aware of when your prospect wants to talk and when he wants to listen. Unlike you, he *does* have the choice.

The four guidelines I have quoted will ensure that the maximum value is gained from your initial discussions. Always ask questions or you will never find out what the customer is really looking for, or indeed, whether he is in your market at all. Not only will you please the customer who wants to talk anyway but you will also be fed with the information you are going to need to submit the most acceptable sales proposition.

Finally, do not fall into the error of believing that because you have had the courtesy to listen to him, he will necessarily want to pay the same attention to you. Remember that your motives are slightly different and he might well not be as good a listener as you have trained yourself to be.

GETTING YOUR MESSAGE ACROSS

By listening to what your customer had to say, you have now acquired the background information to present your case. You know something of the business that he is in, and also something of the way he reacts as an individual. How are you going to use that information to get your message across?

The most important point to remember is to use the approach that suits you. At this early stage, all you are trying to say is 'My name is Mr Smith. My Company is Birmingham Engineering Ltd, and I believe I can offer you something which might be of interest to you.' How you actually say all that is irrelevant except that it must suit not only you but also the person to whom you are saying it. Get it wrong at the early stage of your meeting and you will probably not get the chance to develop the next stages.

While you are at the beginning of the relationship with your customer, *don't* use Christian names. I know it's modern and your kids may well call you Tom, or whatever, but in selling, the use of the word 'Mr' creates the respect to which the buyer feels he is entitled, whatever he may say publicly. He will soon introduce his own Christian name into the conversation if that is really what he wants, but even then don't be too quick with the back-slapping routine. As you get to know your man, you will soon find out if the familiar approach is going to help or hinder you. I am well aware that in certain industries, the construction industry in particular, a Christian name is virtually essential, but in others, such as the insurance business, the prospect is looking to you for sound financial advice which he does not have himself and the respect he has for you, and that advice, will depend on whether you treat him as he expects to be treated. As a general rule, unless you know differently, play it safe.

The art of getting your message across is not simply being articulate, although few salesmen would have great success if they were not. The real art is to shape your presentation *in the form best suited to your customer* and this will vary with what you know about the man with whom you are dealing. But a few rules of projecting yourself will be good for every occasion:

■ **Always speak so that you can be clearly heard** The level of clarity used in everyday conversation is not the standard you need for your selling and in particular you will need to speak more slowly to ensure your message is understood. By slowing down your pace, you will also be in a better position to think ahead on what you are going to say next.

■ **Constantly alter the speed and pitch of your delivery** and show your own enthusiasm with as much variation as possible. A flat voice is not only difficult to listen to but also conveys disinterest on the part of the speaker.

■ **Always aim to look at your prospect** and not at the technical data from which you may be quoting. Maintain this eye contact to retain his attention, dropping it every now and again to avoid embarrassing him. You will also find that by altering your own position, for example by leaning forward, you can help to emphasise an important point.

■ **Don't make use of company jargon** believing that your customer will automatically understand it also. The determining factor on whether something is jargon or not is the perception of the audience, and what is jargon to one may not be jargon to another. However, if he doesn't understand it, he will be reluctant to tell you and you will have set up a barrier which sooner or later you will have to break down again. In many businesses, phrases and words which are everyday language to yourself will be meaningless to the layman who *needs* to understand them before he can recognise the benefits of your proposal.

■ **Stop and ask questions** throughout your sales presentation to confirm that your prospect is really with you. Always make sure that those questions are simple and centre on only one idea. Never combine questions in one sentence as your customer will merely select the easiest one to answer. As Winston Fletcher said in his book *Super Efficiency*, 'It is always worth apparently wasting a few minutes at the outset ensuring you have been understood, to avoid wasting a few days later when it transpires that you haven't.'

■ **Get commitments as you go along** Not only will you hopefully get yes responses (more on that later), but you will draw your prospect into the discussion from the beginning.

■ **Choose your vocabulary with care** Forget all the indefinite words such as 'possibly', 'likely to', 'probably' and 'hopefully' and use positive words such as 'certainly' and 'will'. Replace 'if' with 'when'. All these choices of words will emphasise in the buyer's mind the certainty of what you are predicting. 'Your costs *will* be lowered'. Not 'I think it is likely that your costs will be lowered.' 'When you agree to my proposition' has far more conviction than 'If you agree to my proposition.' In everything that you say, the buyer is looking for assurances that he is doing the right thing, and unless you give him those assurances, he will not only fail to give you the order but will probably fall victim to the next salesman who does.

■ **DON'T tell jokes** — please. Sure, he'll laugh because everyone does, but that does not mean that he appreciates being the recipient, and anyway, you'll be lucky to find someone with the same sense of humour as yourself. Even if you do, your customer will probably reckon that he's better at telling jokes than you are, but most important of all, you will be stamped as a man whose priority is not the business he is promoting and you will not be taken seriously. *Don't tell jokes*.

■ **Steer clear of your own problems** – personal, social or medical. Don't tell your customer. He may tell you about his, but that is his privilege. Keep yours to yourself. As Mark Twain once said, 'Fifty per cent of the people you tell will not be interested and the other fifty per cent will probably be glad.' You are not going to come out on the right side with odds like that against you.

■ **Never argue with a customer** You cannot win. The old saying of a customer always being right doesn't actually mean that the customer *is* always right but it certainly means that you are a fool to argue with him even when you think he is wrong. The customer can always win in the end by buying elsewhere.

IS THE CUSTOMER INTERESTED?

It is important to the way we continue to make our presentation that we should know whether we are securing the interest of our prospect or not and in selling we should always be looking for the moment when we are achieving that object. There is no advantage in pursuing our case if the message is not getting through. Often it is the buyer who has realised before the salesman that there is no place in his life or his business for the proposition you are putting forward. Is there any way we can use the physical reaction and response of our customers to tell us whether we are on the right track or not?

Study body language

Over the last two decades, there have been many attempts, especially by the American influences, to draw into selling the analysis of 'body language', a science designed to gauge the state of play from how our buyers may sit, move or gesture. Unfortunately, as a science it is far from reliable and the fact is that we all have a different way of expressing ourselves in any given situation. However, having said that, it is helpful to recognise some of the signs which *can* indicate how we are being received.

In your selling, you will always need to be on the lookout for wandering attention, and if you have secured the eye to eye contact that you should, any failure by the buyer to maintain that contact should tell you that he is not absorbing what you have to say. A lack of interest is difficult to disguise in any discussion between two people and generally will indicate that the customer has not yet become involved in the presentation that you are making. Perhaps questions which should form part of your presentation are not being put as often as they should, but either way, that presentation needs to be revised to secure the participation of the man you are selling to. However, if annoyance also is creeping in, you can be sure that you indeed have his attention but his reaction has become negative and a negative listener will often react with his fingers, either by drumming them on the table or by a slight clenching of his fists. If, however, you have secured the interest that you want, you may well have the benefit of seeing your customer nod, easily the best and most recognisable reaction of all. Few people nod when they actually mean 'I disagree.'

However, do not always blame yourself when the interview appears to have lost direction. There are always outside influences which can affect any meeting and it is not impossible that, in spite of having arranged an appointment, you arrived at an inconvenient time. You may not have his attention simply because, just as you arrived, an unexpected crisis landed in his lap, or you may have misjudged the time he was prepared to give you. When this occurs, keep wide awake for the signs that you get, and offer to leave him so that he can sort out his more immediate problems. Then make a further appointment, and return when you are more likely to have a receptive audience.

Seek to control the discussion

Assuming your presentation goes as planned and you are securing the attention of your prospect, it is important that the direction of the discussion remains firmly in your own hands. If you have pre-planned your visit properly, you will have gone in with a specific objective that you wished to achieve, and this objective will be more clearly defined if your call is a follow-up call on a previous one. You must always keep that objective in view and, if you find yourself drifting away from it, you will need to redirect the conversation, remembering the inertia of the buyer which presses him to avoid buying from you if he can possibly do so. If the conversation drifts out of control, you will have failed if the customer himself has to bring you back to the object of your visit. The moment that he says to you that he has really talked enough about golf, or holidays, or whatever, and 'what was it you wanted to see me about?', you will be on the defensive, and compelled to finish the interview in his time rather than yours. During the whole course of your meeting, you must guide the discussion so that you open your sales presentation at the time *you* choose and then have available all the time it requires. If you exhaust the time you have with social chit-chat, you could find yourself shown the door before you have achieved what you went there for.

Never forget this cardinal principle, that you *must* guide the format of any selling presentation you make, and lead it the way you want to go. Many salesmen fail to do just that and are unable to understand why they are always well received, always seem to have a good social rapport with their customers but are not able to steer their conversation into the selling routine which gets them orders.

So how should we control that format and work to a pattern which will help us to arouse the enthusiasm of our customer for the product we are promoting? These are the basic principles of selling which we will deal with in our next chapter.

CHECKLIST

- Use empathy in the way you develop your case.
- Ask questions to get your customer talking to you.
- Always listen to what your customer has to tell you.
- Guard against over-familiarity.
- Control what words you use and how you use them.
- Never argue with a customer. *Never.*
- Body language can help – or hinder.
- Always control the direction of the discussion.

5

Discipline your selling

'I am a great believer in luck and I find the harder I work, the more I have of it.'

Stephen Leacock (1869-1944)

I assume that this is probably not the first sales manual that you have read and I hope that you will already be well familiar with the classic principles of selling outlined in this chapter. These rules are nothing new and I believe that no one has yet come up with anything better since the original AIDA techniques were devised. I would suggest that how you actually *use* those principles can be changed and it is that change that needs to be worked on. Any study of selling cannot overestimate how essential it is that you make AIDA a rigid discipline rather than a vague theory which you know but do not regularly apply.

The mnemonic AIDA *must* be the skeleton of any sales argument. For those who are not familiar with the principle, AIDA stands for:

ATTENTION – INTEREST – DESIRE – ACTION

When you are next viewing television, look at any commercial you see and you will see that in all advertising this principle is universally used. The first object is always to attract attention and whilst any method can be used, it must have the effect of drawing in the listener, for it is only when he is listening that what is being said will have any impact. In direct selling, your appearance, your smile or your personality may well be the features that attract that attention. You may get help from visual aids or brochures, but you will certainly not be able to follow on to gain interest if you have failed to secure attention in the first place.

The listener's interest must necessarily be aroused through the details of the service or product that you are offering, the specification you are presenting, and what you are able to show and tell your customer. Your buyer will need to identify with what you are saying, and must be persuaded that it has some personal relevance to him.

His desire for what is on offer is totally different from his interest. We can all have interest in a Ferrari but, because of the price, it will have little likelihood of developing into a practical desire. (If you already have a Ferrari, you probably have no need to read this book in the first place!) The desire you are aiming to generate in your customer means persuading him that he needs your product and to do this he must eventually accept both the detail and the cost of your offer. You will need to develop that desire, by describing the product in terms of specific benefits *to him* rather than in terms of the features of the product itself.

The prospect's main consideration is what the product will do for him and how it will meet his needs. A customer who walks into a chemist to buy a toothbrush does not really want a toothbrush. What he actually wants is clean teeth and as that is an impractical request, he translates it into something he can ask for. He is now open to suggestions from the chemist on how he can best achieve what he is seeking, ie the benefit (cleaner teeth than he has had before), that a more expensive, or even an electric, toothbrush will give him. If that requirement can be met by what you are offering, and it comes within the price range that he considers reasonable, his problem is solved and he will buy. This is why you should never sell the product, *always* the benefit that results from it. You will find that invariably brings in the words 'which means' after you have described the feature which you are presenting, for example, a new insurance policy, *which means* improved peace of mind.

THE BENEFIT TRANSCENDS THE PRODUCT

Before we consider the action part of the mnemonic, consider first a somewhat surprising assertion. *You are not there to sell your products or services.* You are there to show your customer how he can improve his business, how he can improve his lifestyle or how the product or service offered by your company will benefit him in what he does. This benefit will be different for every customer and the good salesman will be able to vary his presentation to ensure that it is tailored only to the customer in front of him. It is of little advantage also to tell the customer the features and benefits of the service which appeal to you. It is only those benefits which have a direct appeal to your customer which will be of any value in securing the business. You are there to offer solutions to a problem and you will never succeed unless you find out first what that problem is.

In analysing the benefits you are offering, do not make the mistake of offering too much choice, even if that choice is available from your stock or the services that you are offering. The buyer will want you to limit his own choice (and his problem of making it) by offering those products or services which have most relevance for him. After all, you are the expert and he is looking to you for advice. Make his choice wide open and you are really offering him no guidance at all. If you do not believe me, ask yourself whether you really like the twenty page menu offered in some restaurants or whether you would prefer to be given a limited but varied choice based on the expertise of the restaurateur. I know that not everyone will agree with this view either, but you are not aiming to please the odd 5 per cent in this world. If you are, you are riding for a fall.

CONVERT NEED OF PRODUCT INTO WANT OF BENEFIT

So why should anyone buy your product in preference to the others on the market? Basically the customer must both *need* and *want* the product for you to succeed. Your prospect may well need your product in his business or home but does he also want it? He may need double glazing but he actually wants a new car. If you are selling double glazing, you have work to do. (Also if you are selling cars but here your requirement will be slightly different!) In his business he may need advertising, but he wants a new carpet in his office. Your job as an advertising executive is to reverse that priority. The more you realise that you are selling primarily needs and then converting them to wants, the swifter you will become successful at the business of selling.

To help in getting your customer into perspective, it is extremely important to discover the benefits your customer will gain (and they will be different for each prospect), because only when you know what they are can you convert those needs into wants. Even a different man in the same company will want to hear different advantages and benefits. Assume that you are selling a new pension scheme to a large company. If you are in at the top and talking to the managing director, he will want to hear of the value it will have to his company standing and to the retention of his staff if he introduces such a scheme. The accountant will be looking far more closely at the costs and how the company contribution can be met within his budget. He will also need to be reminded of the benefits of such a scheme to his tax position. The trade union representatives, if there are any, and certainly the workers themselves, will need to know how it will affect their take-home pay and how this will be offset by the advantages they will gain. Whether it costs their company more cash or less tax will not greatly interest the men on the factory floor, and whether the workers can retire with more peace of mind will not greatly interest the accountant. Exactly the same product but with different interests for each employee. Be aware that it is easy, and fruitless, to sell the wrong benefits to the wrong man.

In every selling situation, we need to emphasise and uncover a demand which every sensible person knows is there, but which, because it is not urgent, is easier to ignore and leave to another time. The customer then requires to have presented to him what the product will do for him (the benefit) and when he is convinced of that and is persuaded that the price you are asking matches that benefit, you can then move on to the next stage of action.

ACTION: SECURE THE ORDER

Action merely means *finalising the business*. It is no more or less than that. Placing and receiving an order involves a major commitment from both sides to bridge the gap between two different points of view. It is the most important part of selling and will be looked at in far more detail in Chapter 9.

So let us look briefly at the basic rules of your negotiating and your methods of keeping the pace going until you secure the order. These rules will, hopefully, give you the right environment in which to make your case and are general pieces of advice which should ensure that your customer is receptive and relaxed and that you are heard as attentively as possible.

THE RULES OF YOUR SELLING GAME

■ **Make an appointment** Aim, wherever you can, to call by appointment. This is a cardinal piece of advice which is probably the easiest of any to ignore, simply because you may know your prospect, you may know that he will see you, and it takes a great deal less trouble simply to arrive and announce your presence. Where you are making your first call, or you consider your prospect of unusual importance, I have no doubt that you obey all the rules and you telephone beforehand to make sure that the time is suitable. If you can, aim to use the same principle when you make regular contact calls on your customers and I can assure you that the likelihood of your irritating the customer on whom you arrive unexpectedly will be minimised. People do have other priorities other than seeing itinerant representatives and even if you are seen, it may well be without the goodwill that you would otherwise have received. Even if you do not have a formal appointment, with the easy availability of carphones there is nothing to stop you making a quick check call on the way to ensure that your prospect is not otherwise engaged.

- **Call with a purpose** Forget 'courtesy' calls. Much more important, forget telling the customer that you are making a courtesy call. A real sales professional will always have a reason for a visit. I can assure you that any sales call, however sociable it seems and however well you appear to be received, will never get into the right pattern until you have established with your customer *why* you are there. He might even be pleased to see you but without a sensible reason for calling he will, shortly after you have gone, be quick to forget you and why you called.

- **Choose the selling ground** Never sell in the reception. There are continual distractions, your buyer is available to any or all of his colleagues who may be passing, and it will be evident that your buyer is not really committing himself to the importance of what you have to say. In addition, your competitor or at the very least, a friend of your competitor, may well be in earshot. Explain all the reasons why you need to talk to him privately in his office where you can have his full attention, even if only on the excuse that you need a table on which to present your case.

- **Get the customer sitting down** Aim to get the buyer sitting down. There is more evident permanence about your meeting if you are seated on opposite sides of a desk. Aim also to sit down yourself. I can assure you that the practice of those buyers who leave their salesmen standing is no accident. They *know* that sales professionals will be easier to eject from a standing position than when they are sitting down.

- **Accept the offered refreshment** *Always* accept an offered tea or coffee even when you don't want one. Initially it will be too hot to drink anyway and will assist in extending the time you are going to get and even after it is cold (and still partially there) it will prove a barrier to your conversation being terminated. Most buyers are basically polite and, having offered you refreshments, will be reluctant to throw you out until you have finished them. It is also no bad thing to share with your buyer his own ten minute break when he is more likely to be relaxed himself.

- **Ignore local interruptions** If a colleague of the buyer comes in to interrupt during your presentation, ignore it. If anyone is going to break the continuity of what you are doing, make sure it is the buyer and not you. You have been given an appointment and at the very least you deserve the buyer's sole attention during that time. If you ignore these interruptions you may well find that the buyer will dismiss them swiftly too. Of course, if the new arrival is a senior member of the company, it is a different ball game and, if he is likely to be concerned in the purchase decision, you may even be able to draw him into your presentation.

- **Check on his buying authority** Right from the commencement, and hopefully before you even arrive in front of the customer, make sure that the man you are talking to has the necessary authority either to buy or to recommend to buy. You may well have to find this out from someone else with the company, as often a junior purchasing officer will be reluctant to admit that his authority is limited. Remember that however good a salesman you are, if the wrong man is on the receiving end, it will all have been a waste of time and it is far too late to ask the question when you are on your way out.

- **Aim for the top man** If there is any doubt at all in your mind concerning who is the decision maker, always aim for the man at the top. At the very least you will never hear him say that he has not got the authority to purchase. You can always go downwards in the authority chain of any organisation but you will find it almost impossible, if you have made the wrong contact, to go upwards. Ask the man you are talking to whether the decision to buy is really his. If he says 'no', then don't waste your time any further. If your contact says that, before making a decision, he has to refer to someone else, that someone else is the man you should be in front of.

■ **Always seek the answer 'yes'** Throughout your presentation you must be asking questions which will need the answer yes. After all, your final question must raise a 'yes' to be of any value, and the sooner you get the principle established, the better. When forming your questions, your empathy and understanding of the customer should tell you whether he is likely to answer no and by doing so build between you a barrier to your sales operation.

■ **Listen to the buyer** During the sales discussion, make sure you sit back and listen to what your buyer has to say. What he has to say is the difference between what he is really looking for and what you are presenting. Can either your criteria, or his, be altered? Find this out and you will know what you have to deal with.

■ **Know your competition very well** Know your competition at least as well as and possibly better than you know your own product. Always be wary of the type of sales management which insists that your sole object is to sell the qualities of your own service. If you accept that you are selling benefits and advantages for your own product, it must be pretty obvious that the competition are doing just the same. It will, therefore, be essential that the benefits that you press are not those claimed by the competition, and it will be equally essential to know what the competition is claiming for its own product. Your customer is going to buy by making straight comparisons between your product or service and that of your competitors, so you had better have expert knowledge both of their products and their method of promoting them. If you can get in first and minimise the advantages which you know will be set up against you, you will have far greater success in establishing the importance of your own.

■ **Tailor the approach to suit the buyer** In your negotiations you must constantly sell in the same way that both you and the purchaser like to buy. Always examine your presentation both as a buyer and as a seller and you can continually adjust what you are doing to make it more acceptable. Always relate your product or the service you are offering solely to the other person. It is part of your training as a salesman that you become able to change gear and alter your presentation as you go along.

■ **Have a specific objective** Always have an objective. In consumer selling, it may well be to secure an immediate order. When selling large capital equipment, it may be to clarify the specification detail. With insurance selling, it may be to secure the information you require to make a proposal. Whatever the business you are in, you need to have a positive goal which you intend to achieve before you leave that meeting. The approach of 'I was just passing so thought I'd drop in' or 'Reckoned you might be here so just came in to say hello' and – the worst of all – 'I'm just making a routine call' are all time wasting approaches, and, to a busy buyer, the last thing he wants to hear. If you do not have an objective before you go in, how do you know when you come out whether you have achieved it or not? *You are chasing business, not chasing customers.*

■ **Give a little — take a little** If you find yourself asked to make concessions on the proposal you are submitting, never agree to any variation without securing some advantage for your own company. A more attractive financial deal, if that is what is being demanded, can always be balanced by an adjustment to the long-term commitment that your company would require. A good buyer will recognise that the concession that he wants is going to cost you money and will not be surprised to find that it costs him money also. Always trade one concession for another. While you are giving something away, there is no better time to improve your own side of the contract.

■ **Analyse objections carefully** It is vital to analyse and handle any objections that you get as carefully as possible. The specific topic of objections will be covered separately in a following chapter, but you need to be aware that it is the job of any buyer to present a barrier to your presentation and you should not immediately assume his objections are real. Never disregard them, since they can even be of value to you, but in the same way do not assume either that they are insurmountable.

■ **Keep the discussion under control** Always keep a tight rein on the discussion and set the pace *yourself.* Never let the conversation drift out of control and in doing so you will bolster your own confidence by knowing that you are leading the customer to do what you want.

■ **Maintain eye contact** Maintain eye contact with your customers whenever you can. This is even more important when you are reading from sets of figures or other data. It is easy for a prospect to lose his personal link with a seller who fails to ensure that what he is saying is also being taken in.

■ **At every stage, work towards agreement** Work to secure the buyer's agreement all the time, even on the smallest points. Note those points down and keep referring to them in your sales presentation.

■ **Prepare written proposals with care** If the type of negotiation demands it, you may well need to confirm to the prospect your proposals so that he can sell the principle to his own senior management. It is the layout of this written proposal which is the ammunition you are providing him with, so ensure that all the points you have discussed are properly confirmed.

In the covering letter you must repeat all the cogent buying arguments you have put forward and which almost certainly have not been fully remembered by the buyer. Remember that the buyer will only present what he is given but if you make it easy for him by providing him with the same sales approach you have used yourself, he will certainly do a better job on your behalf. Write down, during the original discussion, all the points to which he reacted favourably and confirm them back to him when you also confirm the price. The regular mistake is to send a bare quotation when what your customer really wants is a proposal to buy. If there are more reasons in the quotation why the buyer should *not* buy it than there are reasons in the explanatory letter why he should, the whole presentation may well end in the file tray.

Always, if at all possible, take any presentation in by hand so that you can go through the detail with your buyer, but remember that, after you have left, others who are interested may need to read it also and if it is not clear and concise you will not be there to help them through it.

■ **Prepare the buyer for your follow-up** Never conclude any letter (or meeting) with phrases such as 'Please contact me if you have any problems' or 'I look forward to hearing from you when you have studied my proposals.' These pass the action straight back to your customer and become an invitation to do nothing. The action and the next part of the selling operation *must* remain with you. Tell him you will contact him in, say, three days' time to check his reaction, and then secure his agreement to that suggestion. Then, when you follow up the inquiry, he will have no cause to complain that you are pushing him too hard because that is exactly what you said you would do.

- **Review your performance** Finally, after any interview, whether it has achieved the object or not, take time to examine your performance and look at your achievement.

- Did your discussion run smoothly and easily?

- Did you achieve the objective which you had determined beforehand and which you set out to do?

- Could you have improved your presentation, your arguments, or the knowledge that you were asked to show?

- If an error was made, can you avoid making it a second time?

So those are the rules of negotiation. Remember them and use them, but in all your salesmanship never forget either that your sole object of being in front of the customer is to *take his order*. Closing the sale must be the most important part of what we do and yet is usually the most mishandled scene in the play. Later on, in Chapter 9, we will deal exclusively with the rules you must apply if you are to get out with an order in your hand.

CHECKLIST

- **Apply the traditional principles of selling.**
- **Attention: make sure your customer is listening.**
- **Interest: sell the features.**
- **Desire: sell the benefits.**
- **Action: emerge with the order.**
- **Pursue the basic rules for negotiation.**
- **Follow a set plan and achieve a set objective.**

6

Overcoming objections

'Arguments are to be avoided. They are always vulgar and often convincing.'

Oscar Wilde

So far we have dealt with our own sales presentation and with our handling of the customer. We will, of course, throughout the whole exercise, be faced by a buyer who, if he is doing his job correctly, will be raising queries designed partly to secure the information he requires, but partly also to arm himself with the arguments he may need to tell you that he does *not* want your product. Dealing properly with those objections is vital to your success. Without objections your buyer would always buy from the first man who made a presentation.

So welcome objections as an opportunity for you to present your case against the preset ideas which your buyer already has. Most experienced sales professionals would agree that the most difficult buyers are those who will not reply, who will not respond, and who leave you to do all the talking. Objections from a prospect will always give you the indication that you need on how he is reacting to your arguments. It is also worthwhile remembering that the buyer who raises no objections at all probably has not yet generated any interest in your proposals.

THE POSITIVE VALUE OF OBJECTIONS

In the first place, do not automatically assume that an objection from a customer is necessarily a rejection of your own proposals. The customer is essentially saying, 'You have not yet convinced me, you will need to tell me more about your proposal.' Interpreted that way, you have been invited to carry on. When you hear, and you will, 'I do not have any call for your product', 'I cannot afford that sort of money', 'I am already adequately covered with my existing insurance', 'Your advantages do not match up with those of your competitor's', it is essential that you stay in there because so far you have failed to convince your customer of the facts that you need to get over to him.

What you *have* generated, however, is a reaction, and whilst it may not yet be the reaction you were looking for, it will, nevertheless, give you the opportunity to look at the reasoning behind that objection, and try to analyse whether it is valid or not. By using questions and encouraging your prospect to discuss the problem, you may well discover his real reason for not wanting to buy and realise that it had little relation to the query that he raised.

You can also be sure that virtually all the sales objections which are raised can be anticipated by the expert sales professional who knows his product and such a person will not be over surprised when those objections come. By improving your skills in recognising the standard barriers raised by your prospects, you will become more professional in dealing with them. There are many salesmen who never get the opportunity to demolish objections to their product simply because the kind of conversation they have with their customers never reveals what those objections are.

There are three ways that you should look at any objection that you have decided warrants an answer (and remember that not all of them do).

■ **Put the problem into perspective** Propose, if you can, that what he is suggesting is not really a serious problem and minimise its significance in his decision process. If, for instance, your client says, 'I cannot afford additional life premiums at the present time,' your aim must be to put the relatively minimal figures you are talking into perspective against other expenses which he regularly incurs. You are merely showing that what he believes to be a major problem is, comparatively speaking, of little consequence. Depending on your own determination, this is probably the hardest option to choose, as what you are effectively saying is that the customer is wrong. Here you must tread with care. Remember the cardinal rule – *never argue with a customer*. You may well win the argument but you will probably lose the order.

■ **Set advantages above disadvantages** Admit the disadvantages which are being presented to you and use that as a base for presenting again all the advantages which he will gain by buying from you. This is by far your best option and will give you the chance of outlining all your features and benefits for the second time. For instance, to the client who argues that your main competitor is offering a lower nett invoice figure, you must re-present all the specific advantages that you have over that competitor, and show how those advantages justify the additional price that you are asking.

■ **Hint at the competitor's drawbacks – carefully** Aim to find out whether any other supplier is able to overcome those objections for him, and from your own knowledge of that competition, ensure that he is well aware of the disadvantages that such a choice would bring with it. Maybe the alternative course he is considering will bring risks which he would prefer to put to the back of his mind. Make sure that those risks are emphasised so that he realises what buying cheap really means. Here you have to be careful as you will be involved in a minor knocking of the competition which must always be handled with skill in order to be acceptable.

The prospective customer who is looking both for the best value, the best deal, and the most effective solution to his problems will be ready to adjust his own requirements of delivery, cost or specification depending on how well he is satisfied with the other benefits on offer. He is not fixed in his demands because, if he is to succeed in getting 90 per cent of what he really wants, he knows that part of the deal may well be to give way on the remaining 10 per cent. As a seller, you may well fall down on one area of the offer you are presenting, but be sure you can get it back by promoting hard the areas where you *do* score. Selling, and buying, is compromise on both sides. You will not succeed in your selling if you think that a buyer is sitting entrenched with all the advantages, and that you are not. Again I would emphasise that you have, in receiving an objection, failed to convince your customers of the benefits of buying, so go through those benefits again, endeavouring to secure as many yes answers as possible.

Categorising the objections that you receive can be helpful. They will all have been raised for one or other of the following reasons:

■ As a test for the salesman whom the buyer considers to be unprepared or ill-informed. If the buyer considers you to fall into one of these categories, he will be aiming to terminate his meeting with you as soon as he can.

■ He may need to secure more information either for himself or to assist him for the presentation he will later make to his own senior management, his partner in business, or even his wife.

■　He may simply wish to delay a decision which he does not want, or has not the authority, to take.

■　He may well realise from what you have told him that he is eventually going to say 'no' and he wishes to have available all the reasons for saying so.

ISOLATE THE REAL OBJECTIONS AS EARLY AS YOU CAN

The earlier you are able to decide into which of these categories the objection falls, the sooner you can decide how to handle it and eliminate the problem, but until that time, you may well be answering the wrong questions. If, for example, you have isolated the real reason as the last one mentioned above and you can see the order being lost, it will be clear that there is little point in continuing a sales approach which is obviously failing to make any impact. Further benefits which have more relevance to your prospect will need to be outlined or the original ones re-emphasised before you can make further headway.

However, one rule that you must always adhere to is to identify *all* the criteria which are blocking the sale and ensure that you know what they all are before you begin to deal with them. If you let the customer bring them up one by one and then deal with them in the same way, you will give him all the time he needs to talk himself (and you) out of the sale. Once he has listed all the problems, and you have noted them down, you are in a position to make the trial close of 'If I can solve these problems, are we in business?'

Whatever the objection, you will handle it in the best way if you can isolate it. If he should complain that he does not understand certain clauses in a service contract that you are presenting, say 'If I can explain those to your satisfaction, are we in a position to sign the agreement?' If price has been raised (and more on that point later), say, 'Leaving price aside for the moment, is anything else a problem?'

What you are asking for is that your prospect looks at all the reasons why he does not want to buy and so effectively state to you that if you can sort those out, there is nothing else to hinder the sale. Even 'I cannot afford' really means that he does not consider that what you are offering is value for money against his other options of spending, unless he actually means 'I have no money', in which case your market research and the results of your own or your company's research were possibly wrong in the first place.

In any selling, whatever the product, you will find that the objections generally fall into a series of psychological barriers which are part of human nature. People will generally tend to go after immediate and tangible benefits and look at benefits in the future as something which can be delayed until a time when they believe they can more easily afford them. It is therefore easier to sell an instant benefit, such as that offered by a new car, than it is to sell a future benefit, as, for example, the advantages of a new financial investment scheme. Both have objections which will be raised against them, the difference merely being in the adjustment of priorities which will need to be made by your prospect.

For this reason, it is essential to decide at an early stage the motivation that drives your particular prospect. For instance, if he is looking at an expensive satellite television installation, he may well believe that it will enhance his reputation with his neighbours and if that is an important factor in his life, it would be foolish to ignore that factor in your sales presentation to him. As a different example, the selling of life assurance will demand a totally different presentation, since it is not a status symbol which your prospect can show off to his friends. That may not be even a minor factor in his thinking, but until you know how your prospect is going to react, you cannot begin to plan your presentation.

THE PRICE OF THE PRODUCT

Whatever the business or industry you are involved with, and whatever you are selling, there is always one aspect in your presentation which virtually everyone concerned with selling would avoid if they were able. This is the point at which you are asked the price or cost of the product or service. There is an immediate reluctance to disclose the one detail which may well lose the sale and the way that this issue is handled will often control whether you emerge with the order or not. A great deal of work is required on your part to overcome this price fear which can easily kill the sale.

If our products match up to what we are claiming for them, and even if they do not, we must develop the habit of declaring our prices with total confidence in what we are asking. We have spent some time persuading the customer that our specification or service is better than our competitors' and there is no earthly reason why he should expect to be able to buy that service at a price cheaper than those of our competitors. The job of the buyer is rarely to purchase at the cheapest price on the market, but his brief will certainly be to negotiate for the best *value*. If we feel the need to apologise for our price then we have not even convinced ourselves of the quality that we are selling. If the buyer is employed by a company, that company will be looking for a financial offering which both meets all their needs and is competitive. They might be demanding reliability and performance, and maybe, if they are in the retail business, they might set great importance on product acceptability by their own customers, but, whatever the product or service, the buyer will have to balance what additional advantages he is getting against the higher cost you are asking him to pay.

Should a direct price comparison with your competitors be thrown into the ring and you know from your own experience that it is a valid comparison, you must then redirect your customer's attitude back to the benefits by agreeing (what else can you do?), saying that you would assume that price will not be his only consideration when buying, and that you would anticipate that he will also be looking at the detail of your offer. This must generate a 'yes' as a response and you then have the ability to bring the discussion back into the particular features which should give you the sale. All of these, which should be unique to your own service, will necessarily cost more, and having been sold to your customer will help to justify the price difference you are demanding.

The fear of being turned down on price is the reaction of any seller who knows that he has not convinced his customer of the benefits of the service he is offering. Once you know that your service, or your product, has benefits that the others do not have, you can start being proud of the price that you are putting forward because a higher price is what you must necessarily ask for a better product.

SELL ALL THE ADVANTAGES...AND THE PRICE

Remember that you must sell all the advantages of buying your product, and indeed this is the basis of any selling, but before you are successful in securing the order, you must also convince the customer that by paying a higher price, he will also be saving money for himself or for his own company in the long run. If your customer buys solely on price, he must be persuaded that he might well jeopardise the effectiveness of his own operation. It is always unwise to pay more than you need to but it is invariably foolish to pay too little. In the words of John Ruskin, who lived and died in the last century, 'If you pay too much, you lose a little money, that's all. But when you pay too little, you sometimes lose everything, because the little that you bought is incapable of doing the thing it was bought to do.' Convince your customer that the best and the cheapest rarely go together, and that if he must deal with the lowest bidder, then he must also add to his figures something extra to cover the risk he is taking. If he is going to do that, he would be better buying the better and more expensive product or service in the first place.

In handling objections, especially valid ones, whether price or whatever, you will sometimes find it to your advantage to agree immediately with the point that has been raised and assure him you will reply to it in a moment. This is a technique which generally a buyer will not expect and having realised that you are not dismissing the point out of hand, he will then be happy for the objection to be temporarily put to one side whilst you go back to the long term benefits which you have offered. It is, of course, essential that you *do* return to the question that was raised earlier, and ensure that it is you who raises it and not your prospect.

But, whatever you do, *never resent objections*. Unless the sale is a very easy one, an objection will certainly be the first positive reaction that you get, and it is worthwhile remembering that without objections there would be no need for sales professionals.

CHECKLIST

■ Objections are the invitation to re-present your case.

■ Make sure you know whether the objection is real or not.

■ Know *all* the objections before you answer them.

■ Isolate and deal logically with each objection in turn.

■ Understand the reasons why people are reluctant to buy.

■ Have a strategy for the problem of price.

■ The deal doesn't always go to the cheapest option.

7

The angry customer

> '*Warning. Customers are perishable.*'
> **Sign in a Los Angeles store**

You will get angry customers. You will also have happy and satisfied customers but, the world being what it is, you probably won't hear a great deal from the happy ones, and even if you do, they are not going to create any problems for you and your company. But deal ineffectively with the angry ones and, if they can, they will make it their business to harm your reputation in whatever way they are able. Act defensively against a complaint and not only does the problem remain unsolved but you lose the customer as well. Act helpfully and productively and you will not only have a chance of resolving the problem but you will probably also end up with a customer who will be prepared to come back to you again.

COPING WITH THE ANGRY CUSTOMER

Accept the blame

Remember that if you work for the company who created (or sold) the problem, it *is* your fault. Don't blame the sales office staff, the computer, the accounts department or the tea lady because, from the customer's point of view, you are the company and he does not want to know about the others in your organisation who might also be involved. It is also possible that you are only dealing with the customer yourself because he has been buck-passed on from someone else, and when this happens, it is more important than ever that you pick up the problem and deal with it before any further irritation is caused.

Stay cool, be professional

Never, but never, get personally involved. If you do so, your emotions will control what you are doing and you will react accordingly. Never, never, react to provocation. Provocation from a customer can often be expected since he will be more emotionally involved than you (after all it is his money he is talking about), but your reaction must be calm and reasonable. Reply with anger yourself and you will have little chance of reaching the sort of compromise which will be acceptable to both of you.

Your job is to solve the problem and arguing, or insisting that the customer is wrong, will achieve little. Similarly putting your customer down, however tempting it may be, must be avoided at all costs. The customer should obviously be calmed down as swiftly as possible, but in doing so you must also ensure that you do not over-apologise for the problems which your company has apparently created. It is easy to soothe any ruffled client by agreeing with all the criticisms he raises but you are then both left on the same side and selling to him again will be difficult if he believes that you are as critical of the company as he is. However you react, it is always worthwhile remembering that a customer's approach to yourself is normally based on how he is treated by you. There *are* customers who are permanently unpleasant but even these can be dealt with effectively if the reaction from yourself is cool and professional.

Exactly what is the problem?

Find out what the real problem is. Imagine, if you will, that you are selling cookers (I know you don't, but it will help to illustrate what I mean). A customer comes on the telephone to complain that his cooker has broken down. It may well not be the simple problem of the new cooker breaking down, but that it broke down at the exact moment when it was needed for an important business dinner. From your company's point of view one failed cooker is the same as another but every customer will see his own problem in personal terms and especially related to the specific benefits which were offered to him at the time he bought it. Among other things, particularly if that important dinner was ruined, your dissatisfied customer is probably also looking for sympathy. Make sure you know what you are sympathising with, and make sure also that the customer rings off having received the kind of answer that he came on for.

What is the customer's desired solution?

Always find out as early as you can what remedy the customer is seeking. That remedy may well be either impractical or possibly too expensive for your own company to consider and you cannot start planning too early if a compromise is going to be the only real solution. You can be sure that the customer knew before he contacted you exactly what was the best he was looking for and what his own options were. It is as well if you can get that information as early as you are able. Remember that most customers, even complaining ones, are basically reasonable people and while their satisfaction is important, you must still be doing the kind of deal which is the most acceptable for the company which is paying your salary.

Wait until the customer has finished

With the angry customer, there is one piece of good advice which is valid for every occasion, regardless of the substance or strength of the complaint. That is simply to listen and listen again until the person with the complaint has finished. He has certainly telephoned or called to let off steam and if you interrupt before he has actually done so, you have merely saved a little bit for later. Listen, make notes, and absorb the problem, so that at the end you are able to repeat it back to show that you have understood. Interrupt at any point and you are stopping him doing what he called to do. Most prospects will expect you to deal with individual points as they arise but be convinced that if further problems are waiting to be dealt with after you have handled the initial ones, you are merely providing a solution before you are aware of the extent of the problem.

Follow through – follow up

When you take action to resolve the problem, take that action yourself and see the thing through. There is little more infuriating for a customer who has raised a query than to have to recount the whole story to someone completely new. Stay with it to the end and let the customer be aware that one specific person (yourself) has taken the problem from him. Later, if you can, follow up with a telephone call to check that the company has done what it said it would do. This does mean a follow up system, but is a great deal easier than dealing with the same complaint when it turns up unresolved a month or so later.

Take the customer's viewpoint

As with the basic rules of selling, always use empathy to look at matters from the customer's point of view. Not necessarily agreeing with that point of view, but certainly knowing what it is. No company, in its service or its products, gets it right all the time and it does not take much persuasion to convince the customer of that. What he will certainly not accept is any attempt to regard his problem as of less consequence than he does himself.

Complaints and performance appraisal

Always regard a complaint as an opportunity to analyse the performance of you and your company in the field. If the complaint is valid, you will certainly not want it to happen again and an unbiased suggestion of improvement from a customer is something which could well have cost you a great deal of money if you had asked the same thing from your planning team or your research department. It is a surprising fact that the majority of dissatisfied customers just do not complain at all, at least not to you, but neither do they come back for your product a second time. You can be certain, though, that they will tell all their friends and colleagues, with disastrous results to your reputation and chances of future business.

Complaints and the loyalty factor

Remember that the loyalty you will secure from any customer who came in dissatisfied and who went out the opposite is far greater than that of the majority of your customers who never had any reason to complain in the first place. You do not often get the chance to secure that kind of loyalty and it is well worth while giving some time and attention to the opportunity when it presents itself to you.

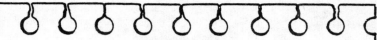

CHECKLIST

- Angry customers will *always* be part of the scene. Know how to deal with them.

- If you can deal with the problem yourself, don't pass it on to someone else.

- Keep your emotional distance. Your job is to provide the solution, not to convince the customer he is wrong.

- Find out the real problem and what solution the customer is seeking. You may otherwise offer more than he needs.

- Use complaints as you would objections. Both are valuable in enabling you to show your own professionalism.

8

How to be a buyer

'A study of economics usually reveals that the best time to buy anything is last year.'

Marty Allen

I must presume that you are reading this book either because you are, or because you want to be, a salesman. So far the book has indeed been all about selling and you might think that I am clouding the issue by introducing a chapter on the strengths and techniques of the buyer.

However, I hope you have already read enough to realise the importance of empathy in your selling operation and to appreciate that the more you know about the man you are talking to, the more you are able to anticipate what he is going to require from you and how he is going to react to what you are going to say. He is a professional, just like you, and if he is doing his job properly, he will be trying to get from you more than you really want to give. What is he trying to do?

THE BUYER AND HIS MOTIVATIONS

A position of strength?

First of all, the buyer would like you to think that he is the one with all the advantages. He can, after all, buy at his own whim and he is unlikely to admit that he does not know what he wants. In reality he probably needs you, or someone like you, as much as you need him. His brief is to act in his own best interests, or the best interests of his company, and to buy a product from which he, or his company, will benefit. It is extremely unlikely that he will do that unless someone who is an expert in that field is able to convince him what that best is. He needs you, and what you have to say may well alter his own initial view of what he wants.

The price imperative

The buyer, in the first instance, will believe that he is going to conclude essentially on price. He does not know the advantages (or benefits) you are going to put forward for your product or service so he has no reason to think that he will have to pay more for them. Again, it will be an essential part of your job to alter the importance that he has placed on price and direct that importance to the added benefits he will acquire by accepting your proposal in preference to the concept he had started with.

Making the best decision

The brief of the buyer is to do whatever is best for himself or his company. If what he does, for price consideration or whatever, results in his doing the opposite to that, he will be taking risks which could eventually reflect on either his own position and well being, or that of his company. He will also know that he is capable of making mistakes in his decision making and will welcome any improvement in his chances of getting it right. The good salesman will convince the buyer that one of the benefits of buying *his* product or service will be to minimise the risks that a wrong decision will bring.

The reversal of tactics

The buyer's tactics will generally be the opposite of your own. If you are wanting to hold price out of the argument until the benefits are outlined, the buyer may well try to force your hand earlier in the argument and make a decision on price before he even knows what he is buying. In the construction plant business where I worked for many years, 'What is your discount?' was often the opening remark – long before even the list price had been discussed. It is difficult to get more illogical than that.

When the buyer is convinced that your service or product, regardless of price, is what he really wants, the price factor immediately becomes less important and consequently easier to resolve. The buyer's job is to get extra discount or the lowest price even after he has decided to buy from you. Get your buying signs first before you start arguing the price and if those signs are strong enough, you may find you do not need to argue at all.

Problems with other suppliers

Don't dismiss the fact that your buyer will often be talking to you because somewhere, with his existing suppliers, he has a problem. Very few prospects have no problems at all with their suppliers, life unfortunately being like that, but unless someone is able to persuade them differently, they will accept a level of mediocrity simply because they are with the devil they know and will be nervous of making any change in case it turns out to be for the worse. The more you are able to pinpoint those problems, either with information from his own staff, or even from the buyer himself, the more you can be positive in assuring him that your own product or service will solve those problems for him. He is looking for benefits and without those benefits being outlined he will probably stay with the supplier he has.

The different types of buyers

- **The friendly buyer** There are always buyers who are too friendly. The buyer's approach will be to direct the conversation away from business and a continual effort must be made to concentrate on the matter which you went in to discuss.

- **The aggressive buyer** The aggressive buyer's approach is often a determined effort to dissuade the seller from offering anything which might take away from the decision he believes is the buyer's only. Such a buyer is often unsure of his own capabilities and he will adopt a domineering response to ensure he is not driven into a decision or change that which he sees no reason to.

- **The indecisive buyer** A listening but indecisive buyer is probably one of the easiest to handle since he has few fixed opinions, and is looking for all the right reasons to make a decision. This is the man for whom you must be well prepared so that you can swiftly provide all the information he needs to agree with your proposal. He will probably give an order earlier than most but, if you fail to secure the order, he will be equally vulnerable to the next salesman who comes along.

- **The overworked buyer** The over busy buyer is a difficult man indeed since he really believes that he has little time either to hear or absorb what you have to say. It is small consolation to realise that others will have the same difficulty in getting through since the busy man's easiest option is not to change his supplier at all. However, once you *are* in here, you might just find that having secured his business, it is the easiest to retain for that very reason.

■ **The argumentative buyer** Lastly there is the argumentative buyer who has possibly had a previous problem with your company. It may even be impossible to make a sales presentation if the earlier complaint was badly dealt with, and particularly if any remedial action is now too late. Complaints that are mishandled will always be the problem of the salesman who has to re-approach for the next business, but buyers change and go elsewhere and the prospect company should rarely be written of just because of the opposition of one man.

All of these buyers will demand a different approach and it is a foolish salesman who believes he can use the same sales presentation for each.

YOU CANNOT OFFER A SOLUTION IF YOU DO NOT KNOW THE PROBLEM

Your prime requirement with any buyer is to find out what he really needs. Is extended credit important? If it is not, you won't overemphasise that advantage with your man. Is he looking for the back-up of a large international group? Maybe his existing suppliers don't match up to that and it has not occurred to him that someone else does. Whatever he is really looking for, it is essential to find out as early as you can. Believe me, your buyer is looking for guidance and if you don't offer it he will see little advantage in changing from the system he has already. The natural inertia of a buyer is essentially because it is easier to do what he has always done rather than pioneer in a new direction. Almost any new decision that is made will cost the decision maker, or his company, hard cash and it will be your initial job to persuade the customer that such money will be well spent.

Work on a bundle of preconceptions about the man to whom you are selling and you will certainly take all the wrong actions on how to deal with him. Yet that is just what the majority of sellers do, and why, as sellers, they often start off with an inferiority complex about the man in front of them.

Always remember that a customer, whether buying for himself or whether buying as an employee for a company, knows first of all that his need is to buy the best *value*. He is not necessarily trying to buy the best (because he may not need it) and he is certainly not aiming, whatever he says, to buy the cheapest (if he was, and he is paid to be a buyer, there would be little need for his own job). He is paid the salary he receives to sort out the wheat from the chaff and to come up with the reasons why your kind of product is the one which will benefit his company most, and then to decide which of the many competitive suppliers making that product is the one to do business with.

The decisions he has to make have got to match up with those basic requirements, and nothing that he decides will justify the easy replies of 'I always get a good proposition from Birmingham Engineering', 'You're too expensive', 'I've always dealt with Tom, have done for years', 'Our existing suppliers seem to give us all the requirements we are looking for'. With objections like that, the buyer is showing that he is not acting in the interests of either himself or his company because even if he appears to be satisfied with what he has got, his job must be to continually evaluate his needs and listen to those people who might tell him that there are better and more profitable ways to run his life or his business.

The target of ensuring that the buyer acts in the interests of his company may well be your first one, and will hopefully get him looking at your proposals in the light of what they can do for him rather than as an unwelcome interruption to the routine that he has been exercising for years.

Remember always that the buyer has a series of options at his disposal:

■ Not to do anything and to stay with the product or service that he has. This may, if it is the wrong product, be costing him money and merely be prolonging that loss. He will need to be convinced of this before he will accept any alternative as a benefit to him.

■ Change what he has, but not buy from you. Here it will be essential that you find out what is his motivation in going to the competition and what benefits he thinks he will have that he will not get from you.

■ He can spend his money elsewhere on a product not related in any way to your own. This is a simple desire/interest choice and, if he does this, you have failed to persuade him on both counts of the attractiveness of your own product.

The fourth option is, of course, to buy from you, and whilst this is the option you are going for, you will find it hard going if you do not work also to eliminate the first three alternatives he has available. However, if you *do* eliminate those first three, he really has only that one choice left.

CHECKLIST

■ If he buys badly, the buyer takes unwarranted risks. Make sure he knows what those risks are.

■ Maximise the advantages you are offering. Minimise the importance of price.

■ If you do not offer a benefit, the buyer's inertia will stop him moving towards you.

■ Look at the options of the buyer. While he is still considering the others, he won't be taking yours.

9

Closing the sale

'Most things are lost for want of asking.'
George Herbert, English poet (1593–1633)

All that has been done so far, whether it has involved persuading the customer to like you, your company or your product, will have little commercial value if you cannot emerge with an order in your hand. It is always far easier to leave without a decision having been made, and indeed, the relief of getting out without a specific rejection almost encourages the salesman to accept a delaying tactic on the part of the customer. However you sell, and whatever method you use to convince your customer, you will find that a decision will never be made unless it is specifically asked for.

THE NEED TO OVERCOME INERTIA

The buyer, just because he is a human being like yourself, will have a natural built-in inertia to change the way he has always done things before you arrived. Even if he becomes convinced that what you are offering will be of great benefit to him or his company (and that is the state of mind you are trying to achieve), there remains the inertia which stops him actually completing the job of ordering. If you fail to ask for that decision you will have given your customer a tailor-made opportunity not to give it to you. Let him get away with that inertia and not only will you walk away without the business you came for, but you will also have paved the way for your competition to walk in and finish the job for you. To overcome the inertia of the buyer, the majority of all buyers need that final pressure which comes with the close, to make them get round to the actual completion of the order.

Many salesmen who believe that they have done everything correctly in proving the benefits of their product are surprised on their next call to find that the customer has ordered a similar product elsewhere, and all because there was a failure to ask for the order. Believe me, if you have done your groundwork properly and you choose the right moment to ask, there should no longer be any reasons left why the buyer should say no. As Ben Feldman says, 'You make the sale when the prospect understands that it will cost him more to do nothing about the problem than to do something about it'. The ability to secure the purchase decision at the same time as you make the sales presentation is the skill which separates the effective salesman from the indifferent. Let us try to make the rules easy.

RULES FOR CLOSING THE SALE

The proposal form in your hands

If you have a proposal form or some schedule which you are hoping to get completed and probably eventually signed, get it out before you actually need it and, if you can, use it during your conversation to complete some of the specification or details that you will require when you do press for the order. If it is the basis of the contract you are planning together, you will certainly be needing it at some stage and that way your customer will get used to the idea of it being there before any decision making arrives.

Secure replies conditional to the order

Aim to lock your prospect into placing an order by saying, 'If I am able to answer these queries to your satisfaction, may I assume that we are in business?' By trading those replies against his order, you are making a trial close against the objections he has made.

Assumptive closing through alternative choices

It is never too early during your negotiations to talk with the assumption that you will be getting the order. It is, of course, a possibility simply to ask for the order, but the question, 'Are you going to give me your business?' is a dangerous one, for if the answer should be 'no', you will then need to go back to first base to re-present your case, and you may well not be given the time to do so. To avoid the problem, you must use different questions to secure the same result and often the Alternative Choice method will lead you in the right direction. For example, 'Are you looking for a higher output or are you essentially looking to improve the quality of the product you are already manufacturing?' makes an answer easy without demanding a firm commitment to the final agreement. Questions and answers such as this gradually lead your client to realise that the final decision is less of a major step than it was before. 'Do you prefer a cash arrangement or our special finance scheme?' is a similar type of question, in that it does not ask for a 'yes' or a 'no', but does secure some agreement to the detail which you have proposed. But design your questions to use only the alternatives between the details of your proposal and, until you feel ready to clinch the actual order, never offer the choice between buying and not buying. You will probably only get one reply if you do.

The disincentives of delay

Try to have available and introduce into your argument a logical reason why any delay in ordering would be to the buyer's disadvantage. The hint of a possible price increase, extra cost to himself while he carries on under his existing system, added profit by investing now rather than in six months' time, are all reasons why it is to his benefit (not yours) to make a swift decision to buy.

Be alert to signals

Throughout your sales presentation you will receive signals from your buyer. Watch out for them and try to identify them. Signals such as 'I must say that I like the option which gives me insurance cover whilst I am away on holiday'..., 'Yes, I do like the fact that your service division is only three miles away'..., 'Yes, I am keen to have added production capacity in hand'.... These are all remarks that indicate the prospect is following your way of thinking.

Similarly, your buyer will raise questions which are signals in the same way and which will enable you to ask further *yes* questions. Questions such as 'Can you give me insurance cover up to the age of 70?' generates the reply 'Yes, we can certainly do that. Is that the particular age that you had in mind?' 'What did you say the measurements are?' **Reply**: *They are 5 × 4 metres. I believe that fits in with your requirements doesn't it?'* 'Are you able to finalise the specification detail in three weeks?' **Reply**: *'Yes, we can meet that requirement. Is that what you're looking for?'*

Use return questions like this whenever you begin to receive the buying signals. The yes answers that you get will be invaluable to you in your final close. But never try to make the close before you get some of these signals, and even more essential, never fail to recognise them and act on them when they are there.

A small decision first

Sometimes, particularly if you are selling an expensive service or proposition, it can help if you are able to secure a decision on a minor point before launching your trial close. 'I assume you will (not 'would') require the optional advantages we offer under Clause 16a?' This will relate to some unimportant factor which will be no major decision for a man who is anticipating spending a considerable figure with your company, and having made that small decision, it will be easier to make the major one which will follow.

Never take no for an answer

Never take a simple 'no' for an answer. You must firstly always know *why* 'no' so that you can evaluate the reasons behind the reply. Only that way can you hope to put forward your own response designed to bring the decision back your way. In most cases the reason you are given is not the valid one anyway. The prospect's wife may have just run off with the milkman, and he is certainly not going to tell you that. There may also be other reasons which he believes will be too easy for you to demolish and it is vital that you find out the real reason behind his thinking. As we said earlier, a 'no' often means simply that you have not yet provided enough information for your prospect to make a decision.

Once you believe that you know why you are getting a 'no', that is the time when you need persistence to avoid taking the easy way out of leaving without the order. As John Fenton says in his excellent book *How to Sell Against Competition* (Pan Books), 'The best closers in this world are children under seven. They are unreasonable, persistent, don't take no for an answer, and by and large they get what they want'. After that age, and through adulthood, they (and we) are conditioned to believe that a 'no' might mean just that and once we accept that, particularly in selling, we stand a good chance of accepting it too soon in our sales presentation. Rarely in fact will you find out all the real reasons why you are not getting the order. If the buyer were honest he might say, 'I am not giving you the order because your shoes and your general appearance are scruffy.' What he will actually say is 'You are too expensive' and unless we try to find out that real reason we will spend a long time arguing against the wrong reason that we have been given.

THE MOST EFFECTIVE RULE OF ALL

So those are the easy rules for making your close, but there is one more that is important enough to stand on its own, since it has to be the most effective rule of all. Often in conversation you will hear someone described as a natural salesman, when what is really meant is that he cannot stop talking. Selling, as any professional will know, is *not* the ability to talk when all others have stopped, but it is the skill both of talking *and* listening. Having covered earlier the importance of letting your prospect talk, I am going to underline the vital importance of choosing the right time to keep quiet. There is a point in your presentation when silence is the best sales tool of all.

Silence puts pressure on the customer and, used skilfully, can lead you right into the sale, but for all that, many professionals rarely use it as a tool at all. You will often have heard it said that so and so 'talked himself out of the sale' simply because that person was unable to recognise from his trial closes that there was no more that needed saying. You will have recognised that you have reached the point where you are able to ask for agreement to your proposal, and having asked, it is essential that you wait for the reply. You have presented the features and benefits that you have to offer, and, in passing the action over to him, you are asking your prospect to raise objections if he can, or accept that proposal if you have presented your case effectively. Continuing talking will only give him extra time to think up more barriers against your presentation. Leaving a silence while you wait for his reply will say clearly that the ball is in his court and the longer the silence, the more likely it is that it will end with a 'yes' and an order. As Elizabeth Bowen said, 'Silences have a climax when someone has to speak.' It does, of course, go without saying that at this stage you will be as sure as you can be that your customer is actually ready to commit himself to your proposition.

You may not hear these exact words but their equivalent is said many times every day; 'I can't take your order yet, I haven't finished my sales presentation.' Don't fall into this error yourself. There is really only one time to close and that is when the customer is ready to place the order. If that should occur before you have even started your outline of the advantages and benefits, then take the order and get out. You may well emerge surprised but I can assure you that you will be a lot more surprised if you insist on pressing on with the remainder of your sales talk and then, by doing just that, leave without the order at all. Equally important, having secured the business you were seeking, don't keep referring to it, coming out with phrases like, 'You will be very glad that you made this move' and 'I am confident you will not regret this.' Once you have the customer's formal agreement on a sale, *anything* else that you add can only act against you. Your customer may already be wondering what he has committed himself to, and, given the chance, would like to add some reservations about how firm that commitment actually is. Continue talking and he might get his opportunity.

If you feel that courtesy demands that you do not immediately rush away, by all means talk about the state of the stock market, or about his prize Charollais bull which he is exhibiting at the County Show, but don't mention the business you have concluded, except possibly to give him your thanks as you go through the door. Discuss the detail of the order and you will give your customer the opportunity to raise new objections which he had not previously considered and you will find yourself starting all over again. Get an appointment, get an order, and get out, is the best set of rules that you can have.

CHECKLIST

■ You must *always ask* for the order.

■ Be aware of the buyer's natural inertia.

■ Trade the order against your buyer's objections.

■ Always assume you are going to get the business.

■ Get 'yes' replies throughout your presentation.

■ If you get a 'no', find out why. You may not have been given the real reason.

■ Use silence as your most effective selling tool.

■ Once the order is in your pocket, don't hang around.

10

Marketing, prospecting and the cold customer

'What is the use of running when you are not on the right road?'
German proverb

It is a basic and obvious rule that to carry out your sales operation effectively, you must be calling on the people who are most likely to buy the product you are offering to them. Possibly a somewhat naïve statement of your ambition but nevertheless one which is the object of any market strategy geared to locating the clients in the first place.

Marketing is not selling. It happens a long time before that and involves first, planning and developing your products so that they are acceptable to the market place, and second, matching those products to the people and the applications where you hope to sell.

As salesmen, you may not have great control of the design and layout of the product or service you offer, but it will be fair to assume that this has been the priority of the managers who run the business you are in, and your experience will probably tell you that this product is geared to what the market says is right. The marketing contribution that you will have to make will necessarily concentrate on looking at all the clients with whom you *can* talk and deciding which of those is most likely to do business with you.

ASSESS YOUR POTENTIAL BUYERS

The principle of dividing your buyers into those who are promising and those who are not, comes under the general heading of prospecting. The buyers we must find are those with whom we are most likely to do business and who will provide us with the most profit when we do so. If we look at the time spent talking to people who, at the end of the discussion, turn out to be those contacts who will *never* consider our products, it is evident that a cast-iron method of eliminating them in the first place would be an extremely valuable asset. There are, of course, no guaranteed methods but there are certainly various factors which might clean up our prospecting act and make it more professional.

Examining any market, it is not difficult to mark up the qualities your potential clients must have in order to bring them into the top band of likely purchasers you are looking for.

Your client must control money

First of all, and possibly stating the obvious, your client must have the money at his disposal to deal with you. Not, you notice, the wish to spend that money – that comes later – but the money itself. You can analyse later in your discussions the priorities he may have in disposing of that income but unless he has the availability of it in the first place, any persuasion you might bring to bear will have little effect. I am not suggesting you dismiss someone with a low income as a non-runner, but the laws of logic will tell you that it should be easier to sell to a high earner rather than to one with limited resources.

The prospect must be accessible

Your prospect must also be a man who you can contact and who will see you. There are people who have surrounded themselves with a barrier and if it becomes very difficult and time wasting to open any discussion with them, you might be better off spending your time usefully elsewhere. Against that, the sales professional who does get through might well be the only one to do so, but it is still sensible to look closely at the time wasted on those who proved difficult to see before you consider it the right policy to aim for the hard to get.

Does he disqualify himself?

There will, in many businesses, be conditions which determine whether your prospect is even a consideration for your time. For instance, in life assurance, if your client sky dives at the weekend, is a trapeze artist during the week, and in addition has a history of alcoholism, you may well be able to convince him of the desirability of covering the risks that he is taking (and with little difficulty at that), but if at the end, you, or your company, cannot produce a cost effective scheme for him to consider you will have had a long and complicated discussion for nothing. If others with less demanding qualifications are available, then at least deal with those others first.

Deal with those who come easiest

The client, if at all possible, should be in the mould that you are, or at least in a mould that you can relate to. By all means spread your net to encompass as many as you can, but you will soon find that there are those who swiftly relate to you and there are those who, because you have less in common, you will find hard work. Before you eventually retire from your career, you will have been compelled to deal with the latter as well as the former, but in the first instance, the best advice must be to deal initially with the ones who come easiest to you. You may also find that one particular industry comes more naturally to you than others, and that by concentrating on that industry you get a snowball effect through the specialist knowledge that you gradually acquire.

The client must need the service

The last and most important point in prospecting must be to find those individuals and companies who have a need for your service. When dealing with individuals where a limited amount of information is available, this is often difficult to assess until we are actually with a client. However, from a distance it should not be too difficult to gauge income (from his job and his position in the company), his liabilities (from the type of home he has), his requirements (from the number and ages of his children) and, as you get closer, his attitude to his responsibilities (from the kind of person he is), and from all the evidence you can gauge the likelihood of his doing business with you. When dealing with a company, the actual need for your service is easier to assess, as a great deal of information should already have been secured before you even make your approach call.

New customers...or diminishing returns?

In many advertisements calling for salesmen, you will often find the phrase 'no cold calling', as if this is some kind of advantage or indeed something which makes the job easier or more acceptable. On the face of it, that might even be true, but beware of the job that carries that sort of incentive with it, because without the ability to cold call and find new outlets for your product, you have lost one of the biggest opportunities to make the range of your customers both more varied and more extensive than that of your competitors.

A great deal will, of course, depend on the kind of selling in which you are involved. If you are selling in a retail or consumer environment, you will have little opportunity of finding new customers at all. Generally your prospects will come to you either through advertising, through recommendation, or they will simply walk through your door because you are the only service in town. Frustrating possibly, because in almost all other kinds of selling, the salesman who is able to increase the number of people who might eventually buy from him or his company will usually be the one with the highest success rate in his company.

Sometimes, of course, it is possible to sit back and rely on those customers with whom you have dealt for years and with luck those same customers might even support you and give you a living until you eventually retire. I say 'possible' because what is more likely to happen is that personnel changes within those companies mean that you will inevitably lose one or two active customers each year, while the launch of a new development from your competitors may well lose you one or two more. Without cold calling you are then reliant on your company's advertising or maybe some telephone selling from your office assistants to replace the customer gaps which have been left.

Later on in this chapter we will develop the concept of using the name of one customer as a lever against the next prospect. It is most important when you are prospecting to extract the maximum advantage from any prospect you talk to, whether he is going to give you business or not. Every prospect can probably give you some kind of launch pad to the next one and you should remember never to be too quick to write off a meeting simply because you have decided there is no direct potential for business. You will usually get some information and may even have the benefit of an introduction to one of his colleagues. You have, after all, spent some time on establishing your own professional approach and it would be a waste if that reputation you have earned could not be passed usefully on to your next client.

PROSPECT — OR FAIL

Regular new business must be essential to any company and anyone who ignores this, or any sales manager who fails to demand it, will eventually have contributed to the failure of the service or product that is being promoted. Call it what you will, cold calling or prospecting, it is both the hardest and also the most rewarding of all the jobs that you are called upon to handle. Unearthing a new customer or, even better, finding one that your competitor thought he had all sewn up, and then seeing it through to a signature on your own order form, will, without doubt, do far more for your ego than taking yet another repeat order from the man who plays golf with your managing director. Leaving all else aside, if the business you have achieved has been by your own efforts from scratch, you will have a far better chance of keeping it going in the future.

So what if you don't like cold calling or prospecting for new customers? There are many who will argue, simply because they don't like doing it, that it is a waste of valuable selling time, that too many negative customers have to be visited in order to unearth the potentially good ones and, anyway, if the company advertised more, there would be no need for any cold calling at all. All partly true, but the fact remains that there are many customers out there who are not particularly committed to any one supplier and if you don't find them, someone else will. I can assure you that if you rely solely on the customers who supply your bread and butter at the present and you do not make prospecting for new customers a regular part of your discipline, then, sooner or later, *you will fail*.

So where do you look and how do you handle the prospecting for new customers?

Yellow Pages – a starting place

Of course *Yellow Pages* or similar publications have a part to play, but they will tell you little about the size or potential of the prospect who advertises there, and whilst I would not decry that source of information as a starter, it would be a foolish salesman who used names and addresses acquired from those sources without checking a little further before spending time and petrol calling on them. All else aside, in the average publication of this sort, the advertisement may not reflect the importance of the customer, the information is likely to be at least one year old when you read it (and was probably commissioned one year before that), and many things can happen to the fortunes and addresses of any company over two years. Having said that, don't dismiss the cold calling technique completely. You do at least see the premises, you can make your own analysis of the company's potential, and at worst, you may well be passed on to another customer in the same line of business who eventually might be of use to you.

Read your industry's journals

In the technical journals related to your own industry you will always find invaluable information that can be used to your advantage. The information will probably be in the form of news which is well up to date and will certainly have been researched by the journal's own personnel before publication. If you belong to one of the enlightened companies who supply you with such publications, then *read them*. If the publications, as so often happens, remain in head office and then wind up on a table in reception, ask them to be sent on to you as soon as the MD or whoever else is interested has seen them. You might even get a silver star for your display of enthusiasm, but you will certainly have at your elbow names of companies who may well be new to you, and at the same time a great amount of information about the companies with whom you already deal.

The local press

Try also researching the local newspapers where jobs are being advertised and where often the company will tell you not only that they are expanding, opening a new depot, installing a new factory or taking on new office staff, but will also probably tell you the name of a contact in that company who might well be a useful source of initial information. Local newspapers can often give the right sort of guide on where business is to be had and where investment is being made for the future. If they *are* investing in people, they might well have money to invest in your services also. Be there before the rest and you should get better than your fair share.

Consult friendly prospects

Probably your best source is to use the friends you already have in the industry and to ask them who you should be calling on. You will be quite surprised how a prospect who maybe does not even buy from you, and who you may rate not too highly in your social list, becomes a different man when he hears you asking for his assistance. The information that he will give you will almost certainly be right up to date and he may well also let you use his own name in making your initial approach to that customer. This, I can assure you, is one supply of information that you cannot afford to ignore and must always be part of your everyday routine, particularly when you meet a customer for the first time but also whenever you meet one of your regular customers. People like to impart knowledge and you will rarely find that the response you get is of no use to you at all.

Check the records

Whatever your business and whatever the environment in which you are dealing, it could pay you to check just how much information is already sitting in the office of your own company. There will be sales information on customers who have been dealt with in the past and where contact has been lost. If you are new to the territory, a check call might just be all that is needed to get your name back on their schedule of potential suppliers.

The irregular call

Probably the one great advantage of any serious prospecting on your territory is that it can be done during all those times that regular customer contact might be less than worthwhile. You might well feel that a call to discuss a purchase would be wasted late on in the day or during the lunch period when it might be difficult to secure the attention of your prospect. Getting information on a new company is as easy at that sort of time as at any other and can even set you up for an appointment later on when you can use the information you have gained to advantage.

MAKE YOUR CASE IN PERSON

When cold calling or making contact with any customer for the first time, you will often find that the man you have identified as the buyer is not available. You will be offered the opportunity to talk to his subordinate or even his secretary, and will, no doubt, be assured that your proposals will be put forward to the buyer when he returns.

Always reject this easy way out of presenting your case. At best, you can be certain that your sales pitch, by the time it arrives where it should, will be watered down to make its success extremely unlikely, and at worst it will not make it at all in front of the man who can make a decision. You might well have gained a little useful information towards a further call but you can be sure that on that next call you will *never* get beyond the man you talked to the first time. If you are offered an alternative interview which you know is with the wrong man, reject it and withdraw. It will be far better to start the whole operation again, and probably easier to make the proper appointment when you try for it the second time.

You may even be asked to give literature to the receptionist who assures you 'she will make sure that Mr Spriggs gets it.' Believe me, your literature, or whatever, will be wasted, firstly because no selling is as easy as that, and secondly, even if your literature *does* make its way to the right desk, it will rarely be read without your encouragement to do so, and when you do ring later on to check out the interest generated, your customer will be able to respond that he already has all he needs to know about your service and 'will contact you should he wish to talk further.' Don't leave literature when you haven't seen the prospect.

However, don't lose sight of the fact that with cold calling, for all its disadvantages, you can often follow through with an immediate appointment or an interview. While this may well not be the best way to make contact, as you are working somewhat uninformed and at a disadvantage because of that, you might just have arrived at the right moment when, because you are there, you can offer something that the competition cannot. Leaving all else aside, success like that will certainly restore your confidence in the potential of cold calling rather than taking the alternative of spending an hour in the local coffee bar.

Prospecting is hard work but so is finding the regular supply of new business which is required by any company. By maintaining a regular input of new contacts you can have a reasonable assurance that you will get, not only the business from the new companies who have started up since you last checked out the territory, but also the business from those companies who have, in the meantime, become disenchanted with their existing suppliers and are merely waiting for an alternative option to present itself.

Remember above all else that cold calling is not popular with ninety-nine out of a hundred salesmen and if you can be the one in that hundred who can handle that type of prospecting, you will have a valuable edge over all the rest.

CHECKLIST

- Marketing is *not* selling.
- Separate the good potential from the not so good.
- Use your first customer contact to find the second.
- Cold calling is *not* all a waste of time.
- Where to find the new customers.
- Never deal with the deputy decision maker.

A telephone at your ear

'*I don't mind being put on hold but I think they've got me on ignore.*'

Troy Gordon

Throughout history, the latest inventions have invariably been treated with a surprising indifference and a lack of appreciation of their potential value in the market.

Towards the end of the 19th century in Boston, USA, the manager of the Massachusetts State Bank was shown, and rejected, a revolutionary item of office equipment which could have altered the entire concept of his banking operations. History records him as saying, 'Would you please remove that toy from my office', and certainly, when he used those words, there is no way he could have foreseen how his successors in the bank would use that same toy. It is doubtful also whether Alexander Graham Bell, for he was both the salesman and the inventor of the equipment, could have realised how his new telephone was to change the face of communication throughout the world.

Up to that time, and indeed for many years later, business communications were haphazard and were conducted either by personal meetings or more normally by letter. Suddenly a sales tool had arrived which, used properly, offered a new type of customer contact which hitherto had been impossible. One hundred years on, our customers, and indeed ourselves, are now open to a kind of intrusion which, whether we accept its advantages or not, has altered the way we are able to make contact with each other. Add to that the increased accessibility of our customers who now carry mobile phones, and we would be foolish if we did not alter our selling practices to match the changes which have taken place.

In our professional selling, do we in fact make proper use of the equipment which we have been given? Indeed, when we use the telephone in place of direct contact, should there be differences in the way we communicate with our customers? Why do the majority of salespeople fail to make use of it in the way that they should? It is a fact that the telephone gives a more immediate method of access to customers than almost any other, as no matter what we are doing and often regardless of the fact that we are already in direct conversation with someone else, we always give a ringing telephone our swift and immediate attention.

EFFECTIVE USE OF THE TELEPHONE

If we accept that the telephone *does* give an important edge, and because it is also an expensive sales tool, it is essential we learn to use it effectively, whether we are using it as part of our normal selling operation or whether, as is sometimes the case, it is the way that all the selling within our company is handled. Telephone selling demands a reworking of many of the traditional sales techniques of face to face selling, as many people regard it – wrongly – as equally effective as dealing face to face. The problem is, of course, that on the phone you are working blind and you will be without many of the visual advantages that you would have otherwise.

Telephone selling, even when it is merely concerned with making appointments for a later sales meeting, is one of the hardest methods of projecting yourself, simply because your skills are limited to the use of your voice and personality, and you do not have the same visual advantages that you have when you are sitting directly in front of your prospect. There are, however, ways of training in telephone techniques and of developing the limited senses that you *can* use, so that you are both professional and effective. Used well, the telephone is certainly the most economical way of making contact with the largest number of people in the shortest time.

The following guidelines will be useful.

Plan every single call

Every telephone call that you make must be regarded as a separate sales operation in itself, just as if you were calling in person. Plan it beforehand in the same way, have an objective in the same way, and see it through in the same way with attention, interest, desire and action. If you treat the telephone call as if it is some lesser kind of selling, that is just what it will turn out to be.

Talk to the right person

The essential factor of ensuring that you identify the right contact to talk to is equally important as in your direct selling, but remember that on the telephone there may be even less indication that you are talking to the wrong person. Make sure right at the start that your buyer has the authority to buy. Ask the question if you have to, but even then, don't always rely on the response that you get. There are many people who do not like to admit that the authority for purchase does not rest with them. It might be as well to bear in mind that if you are proposing insurance to a husband and wife, you could find that a joint decision is essential, and that, to avoid your having to repeat the whole presentation a second time, any meeting you arrange will need to include both parties. Similarly, if the works manager cannot buy without a sales presentation also being made to the main board, then ensure that everyone available is in on the act before you commence.

Concentrate on the conversation

As a golden rule for any telephone conversation you make, always give your customer your full attention. Forget what is on your desk in front of you and the next problem with which you might be dealing. At best you will only have minutes to make your point and while you are doing so he will need to believe that he is the most important topic on your mind.

Keep to the purpose of the call

Always keep to the forefront of your mind the reason for your call and don't waste time on social chit-chat. The object of using the telephone in the first place is to make better use of your selling time than would be achieved in a face to face meeting, and this aim is destroyed if all that takes place is a pleasant social conversation with the main objective forgotten. In addition, two minutes of idle talk on the telephone will, to your prospect, always seem much longer than a similar period across his desk, and with his mind geared to listening to what you have to say, if what you *do* say appears to have no substance, he will not be long in telling you so.

Speak clearly

When you speak on the telephone, always enunciate clearly and do not telescope your words together. The recipient of your call will not have the advantage of seeing your lips and you might be surprised how much, in our normal conversation, we are able to comprehend visually when we cannot hear the words that are being said. Concentrate on speaking clearly and slowly, giving yourself time to plan what you are going to say next.

Choose your words carefully

In your everyday conversation, the words that you use are obviously important and will give your presentation style and character, but, on the telephone, those words become far more important simply because you are limited by the senses you are able to use. The following brief rules will assist you in making sure that your words have the most effect.

- **Eliminate words of indecision** The 'might be' and the 'I think' both indicate to the hearer your own doubts. Use instead positive phrases such as 'It is' and 'I know'. The latter will project the firm image of a man who knows his own mind. Talk of his order or his commitment in terms of *when* rather than *if* and always assume that you are going to get his business.

- **Aim to eliminate the cliché phrases that you use in your normal conversation** In place of 'a vast quantity' say 'many'. The meaning is the same and the second, as well as being more decisive, will get your message across in a shorter time. As Winston Churchill used to say, 'Never use two words when one will do. Remember that two words heard correctly are far better than four words which are not heard at all.'

- **Speak to the person, not to the phone** Imagine the person who is listening to you at the other end of the line. This involves hard work in order to visualise a personal face to face meeting but is essential if you are to secure the rapport you need with your customer.

- **Link the customer's views with your own** Using words such as 'we' persuades your buyer that you are on his side. If you have secured his confidence, 'We can solve this problem together' will help to persuade him that he is not on his own. In addition, use the customer's name whenever you can. This will help to make the conversation more personal.

Sound enthusiastic

When you speak, say what you have to say with enthusiasm. Make your phrases flow, avoiding long pauses which always indicate that you may well be feeling your own way. Constantly vary your pitch and try to show your own excitement and confidence in the tone of your voice. On the telephone, even more than in a face to face interview, any lack of interest on your part swiftly becomes evident and a flat voice will be interpreted as a lack of confidence in what you are selling.

Encourage the customer's response

As early as possible in your presentation, make sure that you get your prospect to contribute to the conversation. By getting his involvement, you will avoid him feeling that he is being lectured to or pressurised.

Prepare a checklist of discussion points

Before you make any telephone call, list out the points that you wish to discuss, and make a note of the queries that you expect to be raised so that you are better prepared to deal with them. There are few people who are able to remember, without some kind of checklist, all they have planned to say and it is frustrating to find when you have rung off that the one point you have forgotten was the main reason for your call.

Smile and project confidence

You will find that your confidence will come across in the most effective way if you aim to smile whilst you are talking. Your customer will usually be able to tell when the person on the other end of the telephone is smiling and his immediate reaction will be the same. Even changing position, for example by standing up, will vary the tone of your own delivery and give a different effect to your listener. Always imagine, if you can, that you are facing your customer across his desk and act in the same way that you would under those conditions.

Recruit the 'yes' answers

Phrase your questions in such a way that you will always get *yes* answers. It is always important in any selling to generate those 'yes' responses since a succession of 'no's makes it a great deal easier for your buyer to phrase the final one which will unsuccessfully terminate your conversation.

Remember to sell the benefits

Describe the features of your service or proposal by all means but never do so without promoting your sales benefits in terms of advantages to your customer. Those advantages are what you are actually selling. For example, do not merely say, 'This is the type of insurance policy which can be adjusted each year to suit your changing circumstances' but say 'This is the type of policy which can be adjusted each year to suit your changing circumstances, *which means* that you do not have to commit yourself in the early stages to money which you are not sure whether you can afford.' In an engineering application, your advantage might well be that the production capacity of your machine is well in excess of the prospect's immediate demand, *which means* that additional costs will not be incurred in the future when that increased demand is required. By emphasising the benefit, the buyer can immediately relate to what he will be securing for himself, ie not an impersonal insurance policy or a new piece of equipment, but the peace of mind which comes from it. *That* is the difference between selling features and selling benefits.

Keep a note of points discussed or decided

One point of particular importance is that on the telephone it is always more difficult to remember what has been said than it is when you are looking at your customer. Again, the visual contact in a personal interview helps in logging the salient points in your memory but on the telephone you don't have that kind of assistance. Always record the detail of the person you are talking to, what you were talking about, and indeed what you may have decided. It can often be very difficult later to recall who said what, and much more important, what you have promised to do for your customer. Don't rely on your memory to see you through.

Get the order

Most important of all, always conclude by doing what you set out to do. Hopefully it will be to secure an order, it may be to accept a refusal if that becomes inevitable, or alternatively if you cannot get an immediate order and your prospect remains active, you will need to secure a commitment from him as to the next step he will take.

Take my word that your telephone manner will greatly improve if you remember and make use of all the above rules. You will be able to plan your outgoing calls in a better way and make the most effective use of the telephone costs you are incurring. Try to remember that the telephone is not just a cheaper option to your direct selling. Used properly, it can often also be a better one.

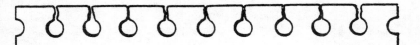

CHECKLIST

■ Telephone selling *is* different. Make sure you know why.

■ Always use your AIDA selling discipline.

■ Identify your prospect and make sure he *is* a prospect.

■ Always know the reason for your call.

■ Get the customer talking and secure his reaction.

■ Retain a written record of what has been said.

12

The skilful use of letters

'Thank you for your extremely long manuscript. I shall lose no time in reading it.'

Benjamin Disraeli (1804-1881)

In all well run companies, a great deal of attention is constantly given to the effectiveness of the sales presentation and to the proper training of their sales personnel. Few would question that training of this nature is essential to make best use of their salesmen, but, when it comes to similar training to encourage sales administrators and others to write effective and persuasive letters, there appears to be a void and an apparent unwillingness to recognise this equally important need. As a result, badly written, ambiguous and ill-prepared letters are very often the norm.

EFFECTIVE SALES LETTERS: THE BASICS

If you can learn to write your letters well and clearly, and produce them with the same empathy that you use in your own selling, they will be effective. All letters which aim to sell must have the same dynamism and life that you have taught yourself to have. They must generate the interest which is part of your sales presentation and must emphasise all the features and benefits that you are offering. There is no reason why sales letters should be any less effective than your direct selling style. Write letters ignoring all these factors and you would be better off not having written them at all. And yet the majority of letters that are sent out by companies are generally illiterate and misspelt, often unintelligible at the first reading, and more important of all, they did not do what they set out to do. The reaction of the recipient who may have written with a query, is often, 'But that was not what I asked' and yet, because you are not there, you have little chance of knowing the reaction that your letter generates.

Whatever you are trying to say, as in selling, you have an object in view. It may be to ask for payment of an account, it may be to reply to a complaint, it may be to solicit business, but if it fails in that object it will have proved an expensive waste of time and may well have killed the chance of doing it properly the second time around.

Unfortunately bad composition, bad spelling and ungrammatical English are no longer considered as major faults in the education of our children and as a result they are often considered equally unimportant in the everyday operation of companies. With internal company memos you might think it no great loss except possibly aesthetically and in the lack of clarity, but if the same carelessness happens with sales letters, then it is maybe time that encouragement and training should be given to make those letters more effective.

I am not going to deal in detail with the basic format of letters. There are, of course, ways to address Kings, Earls and Bishops and there are many tutorial books which will tell you how to do just that without upsetting the laid down system. However, I am assuming that your business letters will rarely be sent in that sort of direction and there should indeed be little problem on how to commence your letter in the first place.

THE GENERAL APPROACH

The rule really is simple. Aim to make your introduction one stage more formal than you would in conversation. If you call your buyer Brian, then 'Mr' is not out of place. If you call him 'Mr' then 'Sir' is not out of place. He might possibly consider you old fashioned but he will certainly not be offended. Do it the other way round and not only might he take offence but others who see the letter could well assume that the letter is too matey to guarantee an unbiased decision when the order is placed. If you really feel that you are making matters too formal by reverting to 'Mr', then address the letter to the company (when you will follow on with 'Dear Sirs') and then mark the letter 'For the attention of Mr Brian Drinkwater', or whatever. The second obvious point is to make sure that the name (and initials) are all correct. It is not difficult and may even require a check telephone call, but if you cannot get his name right then he will probably assume that you know, and care, little about himself and his business. Remember that even in a letter, you are trying to impress the customer with your efficiency. Don't wreck that chance before he even reads what you have to say.

THE TEXT OF THE LETTER

The wording of the body of the letter itself is obviously the only reason for writing it in the first place and is also the area where all the real mistakes are likely to be made.

In the first paragraph, always summarise what has gone before, whether in correspondence or in a meeting. If the letter is an initial approach, explain why you are writing at all. 'Thank you for your letter of 7 November' may sound all right to the recipient if he only writes or receives one letter a month but if someone else picks up the letter, that person will have no idea what that letter of 7 November involved or how important is the reply to it. A brief summary of the situation, a reminder of the complaint, a reference to an order or a proposal, will put the letter into perspective. For example, if it is a complaint to which you are replying, then summarise briefly that you understand that he has a problem, the details of which are as follows..., and that you appreciate that he is looking to you or your company for a solution.

The body of the letter must state clearly what you are going to do, or maybe what you are hoping to achieve. Numbered paragraphs assist in referring to detail later and help also to keep the specific problems or points separate. Separating off detail in this way is particularly useful where the customer writing in with an inquiry (or complaint) may well have rambled from paragraph to paragraph with little logic. By setting it out properly and paraphrasing what has been said, you will be able to clarify in the customer's mind what he is actually looking for.

GUIDELINES ON COMPOSITION

In this short chapter, there is really not enough time to give an elaborate rundown on how to write. Most of us have spent many hours at school and possibly later at University and if we have not got it right after all that, a three week crash course is not likely to make much difference. However, there are always improvements to be made and the following guidelines should help you along the way.

■   **Avoid padding** When writing a business letter, avoid the padding which you would probably place in a personal letter to a friend. Indicate everything you need to say, then slim it down to as few words as possible, and once you have done that, terminate it. If it is difficult to read because it drifts somewhat aimlessly, it will certainly not achieve its objective.

■ **Be specific** Use the words that mean what you want to say. If you promise to deliver 'before the weekend', that means by Friday. It doesn't mean Saturday afternoon (which will upset your customer) or the following Monday (which will infuriate him). If you say that you run a 24-hour a day service, don't be surprised if he rings you up for just that at 3.00 am. Read your own letter before you send it to make sure that someone else's interpretation is going to be the same as your own.

■ **Use plain English** Choose short words which are crisp and to the point. Long words are difficult (for some) to absorb and the really long over-created words (like that one) are not English at all. Believe me, journalese and gobbledegook are not confined to the Civil Service. They are also alive and well in the majority of industrial letters. 'In an efficient manner' is merely a heavy way of saying 'efficiently'. A simple construction implies honesty and being easily understandable is more readily accepted than something which needs to be read twice before it is understood.

■ **Keep it simple** Construct simple sentences which have one basic idea in each. Include them in paragraphs which have one general idea in each. Customers and others who are going to read what you have to say, may not have the time (or the intelligence) to understand a long, rambling, or badly written letter. There *are* people who cannot understand letters just as there are people who cannot write them. If you really cannot say what you have to say in a simple format, it will probably be better for you to make an appointment and go and see the customer (or else get someone else to write the letter for you).

■ **Avoid cliches** Avoid clichés if you can. Clichés are merely words which have been worn to death by others. The moment you say 'Our products sell like...' your reader will, without going any further, be able to say 'hot cakes'. The originality which might well have held your customer has gone. If you don't know what a cliché really is, just listen to the conversation in the average pub and in the first five minutes you will hear 'At this moment in time', 'You can't win 'em all' and 'Personally, for myself, I think that...'. All these are examples of unoriginal thinking.

Similar phrases were, up to a few generations ago, used also in correspondence and a reliable indication of the amateur letter writer will be found in his use of those words and phrases which are wrongly believed to be business 'standards' and therefore always to be used. 'Herewith enclosed', 'Further to our recent communication', 'Following our deliberations', 'We beg your indulgence' are all phrases which you would never use in conversation to a friend and are as out of place on paper as they would be person to person. At least 'We beg to remain, your most obedient and humble servant' and 'We thank you for your letter of the ultimate' have now gone, leaving us only with the acceptable 'Yours sincerely' and a few others. In the words of an anonymous writer, 'Avoid clichés like the plague'.

■ **Be as brief as possible** If your letter exceeds one page, *it is too long*. The second page of any letter rarely gets read with the same enthusiasm as the first, particularly if it is all stapled together. You have only to look at the way it is held while it is being read to see that the pages underneath are getting scant attention. Certainly, no-one would listen to you talking for the same length of time without interrupting. It is a well quoted fact that a short letter is probably more difficult to write than a long one but if it is going to be more effective, then the effort is worthwhile. If it is essential to include further detail, add that detail in an attached list or an appendix.

■ **Courtesy costs nothing** Never be rude in your letters. Not because it indicates that you probably are an offensive person but simply because it will have little effect apart from irritating the man you are writing to (and you will not have the pleasure of actually being there when he receives it). What it certainly will do is to ensure that any concession or agreement you may later be looking for will be far more difficult to achieve. By all means, make your letter sharp and effective, but if it is rude it will get little attention, except possibly later in the law courts. Leaving anything else aside, the worm often turns and the man who was neglected when he was struggling (or owed you money) may one day wind up as the chairman of a company whose business you need. Courtesy costs nothing except when you forget to offer it.

I can assure you that the Christian principle of turning the other cheek may not be particularly pleasant but in business it can even secure the positive response that you are looking for. Often, in a face to face meeting we say things which two minutes later we regret. When writing a letter, we have that two minutes and we should use it as effectively as we wished we had when we were in conversation. The advice to wait twenty four hours before sending a critical letter is good advice indeed and rarely will you send it the next day in its original form.

■ **Retain the initiative** Lastly, in any communication, always finish by retaining the initiative and saying what you will do as the next stage of the action. Leaving a customer to contact you when he needs further information is a guaranteed way of ensuring that you will never hear from him again. Many sales founder simply because the salesman, having gone to all the trouble of finding out what a customer requires, and having followed it up with a letter or quotation listing out that requirement, then fails to realise that the next move to secure the order is *still* up to the seller.

CHECKLIST

■ Use empathy in your writing. Imagine how your letters will be received.

■ Make your letters specific and to the point.

■ Choose and use words that are crisp and simple.

■ Avoid clichés and jargon.

■ Keep your letters down to one page if possible.

■ In your correspondence, never be anything but polite.

■ Always retain the initiative for your next action.

13

Exhibitions and demonstrations

'*The finest mousetrap in the world will not sell unless you take it to the people.*'

Brian Hansom

There are many industries where an effective demonstration of the equipment being sold is vital before a prospect can even evaluate its potential. Obvious examples are photocopiers and other office equipment, but in many other fields also, a visit with the prospect to an existing user is the only way that the salesman can effectively show the capability of his product.

Those occasions where demonstrations are regularly used properly are probably only matched by the times that a demonstration has irrevocably killed the chances of a sale and any future business with that customer. In fact, when you are asked to set up a demonstration, you should always be extremely wary, first of all concerning the reasons why you are doing it at all, and secondly whether what you are doing, and the way you are doing it, is more likely to harm your sales pitch than to improve it.

You might think that this is all very cynical but I can assure you that a product demonstration in the wrong place, at the wrong time, to the wrong audience is a sale irretrievably lost, and yet many demonstrations are set up in just those conditions simply because it is easier to agree to the buyer's request than to set it up either in your own environment or at the premises of an existing user.

KNOW WHAT YOUR CUSTOMER IS REALLY SEEKING

First of all you really have to check out why the customer is asking at all.

Remember from your knowledge of the buyer that his natural resistance to *any* change will be leading him to delay making a decision to purchase, and a request for a demonstration will certainly assist in that delay. As with your technique in dealing with any objection to a purchase, you must always evaluate the background to it and, if you are able to do so, use the trial close of 'If I am able to prove to you that my machine will do the job, are you prepared to make a decision to buy?' That at least tells you the value of the buyer's request to set up the demonstration at all. The alternative question of 'Can I show you what the machine does?' will secure nothing for you except a series of ineffective presentations to disinterested customers who may well be seeking the quickest way of showing you the door.

Initially, you must discover exactly what it is that the customer is looking to prove. Maybe he is in the market for a copier to replace his existing machine, but unless you know that his present problem is continual breakdowns due to inexperienced personnel using that machine, you will demonstrate nothing by showing him your machine in the quiet of his own office. You will merely finish the day by his saying, 'Yes, but I am not sure that it will be right for the application that I have.' Better in those circumstances to find someone who once had that problem, and, as a result of using your equipment, has it no longer. You are then in a position not only to take him to that location (at no great cost to you or your company), show him a machine which has been operating effectively for some months, and let him talk to the personnel who bought it in the first place and who use it everyday. The sales pitch will be done for you since few people will admit to having made a wrong purchase decision, and anyway, one presumes you will have done some homework first and checked out the working conditions to ensure that they are happy with what they have got.

If you *do* use that approach, always make sure that you leave the existing customer and the prospective one on their own to discuss both the machine, you, and your company. It is good advice to make it obvious that you are leaving the group for that specific reason to give them a free run to talk between themselves. Unless the performance of the equipment has been a complete disaster, the few problems that might have occurred will normally be more than balanced by the good features which will be attributed to the machine.

THE RULES FOR A SMOOTH DEMONSTRATION

However, I am well aware that a 'set-up' demonstration often becomes essential and indeed it may be that the kind of equipment you are selling demands it. You must then make sure that, as far as possible, any risks of failure are eliminated before you start.

- Make sure that the demonstration is geared to the application of the prospect, and is not, except by chance, the same type of demonstration that you have given to the previous customer. The two customers will have different demands for the same product and it is of little advantage if you treat them all with the same approach. For example, a copier might have the fastest print time in the business, it might be the most idiot proof machine on the market, or it might be the only one with 24-hour a day service from a local depot. All valuable qualities, but you must, as in all selling, see the demonstration from the customer's point of view, recognise which of those qualities he really will buy on, and present your demonstration accordingly.

- Obviously it is essential that you check out all the equipment that you are likely to need during your demonstration. Trust only in your own judgement, and not in the engineer who is convinced that the power cable is more than long enough to reach the nearest power point. If petrol or diesel is required to make your demonstration model work, then make sure you know where supplies are if the demonstration goes on longer than you planned. If you are demonstrating the capabilities of a forklift, you will not get far without something worthwhile to lift. If the routine you have planned is continually being broken by events you have not planned, you will not only lose the interest of your audience but you will also have blown the opportunity of doing it again. If you tell me that you always do this automatically, then I must believe you, but reluctantly, since in my business life I have had many presentations made to me where the equipment on offer was not only faulty, but obviously so. In some cases the salesman even had to apologise for a problem which he advised me had occurred before.

- If the equipment you are demonstrating, whether it be a bulldozer or a copier, is normally handled by a skilled operator, *never* let your customer, unless he has similar skills (and probably not even then), handle the equipment for himself. I know he will want to, but whatever he does, the machinery will not perform as slickly and effectively as it should and performance is what you are trying to sell. If you do let him handle it and for one reason or another he makes a mess of it, he is certainly not going to blame himself and before you know where you are you will be selling a piece of equipment which is 'difficult to control'. Be warned.

■ Always let the demonstration speak for itself. By all means describe beforehand what the machine is going to do, and talk afterwards about how well it did it, but carry on talking during the demonstration and you will have taken his attention back to yourself and destroyed the object of laying on the demonstration in the first place. He can listen to you in his own office when you both return, but he cannot give his mind both to you and the equipment whilst it is being displayed.

■ Finally, always treat the item you are showing or demonstrating with great respect. Treat it casually and you will lower its value in the eyes of your audience. Treat the demonstration typewriter roughly, bang with your fist on the front of the coffee machine, or even fail to show respect to the computer you use in your own projections and you will find that your audience will treat it with the same disrespect that you have.

A DEMONSTRATION REQUEST MIGHT BE MORE NEGATIVE THAN POSITIVE

For all the comments I have made above, do not dismiss the demonstration as a useful tool of your trade because often that is what it can become. Remember, however, that it is also the tool of the buyer who will ask for a demonstration when he cannot think of any other conceivable reason why he should not buy and who is hoping that a demonstration will provide that negative reason he is looking for. If you don't get the demonstration right, that is probably just what it will do.

The value of exhibitions

So far as exhibitions are concerned, as a salesman you will probably find that these are organised for you and your involvement will be one of attending and selling to the best of your ability in an unfamiliar environment. That environment will be different for many reasons, not least of which is the fact that the customers come to you rather than the other way round, and it is as well to discuss whether this difference demands a different sales approach than you would use on territory.

The fact that the customers come to you is an advantage. Apart from some persuasive work on your own customers, there is little you can do to get the prospects on to your stand, and your main skills will concern how you handle them when they *do* arrive.

The second point to consider is that all those visitors who you do *not* know, and hopefully there will be many, will be people you have not met before, and whose strength either as individuals or companies is completely unknown to you. Consequently you are starting your sales approach with none of the information which you would normally expect to have at your elbow. An early evaluation of those visitors is going to be of prime importance if you are going to use your exhibition time usefully.

Finally, the follow-up after the exhibition may not, either because of territory or knowledge, be your own responsibility and it will be an essential part of your exhibition discipline to record what you have gleaned from the prospect so that whoever does follow it up has more that the usual vague comment that someone called and a general discussion ensued. Believe me, this is very often the way of recording visitors to exhibitions and as you will probably also be on the receiving end of someone else's inefficient recording, you will swiftly learn how that approach can waste the time and cost of setting up the exhibition in the first place.

As an exercise, when you are visiting an exhibition, try passing yourself off as a prospect and gauge the professionalism of the response that you get. The nature of that response will almost invariably be based on the view of the seller and is usually represented by the 'Can I help you?' approach, a question which, I need hardly tell you, can only encourage a 'No thank you' reply from the prospect and a termination of the contact between buyer and seller. Rarely will the initial introduction include a question to provide the answers that the seller needs to know before he can even begin talking about his product or service.

LISTEN TO YOUR CUSTOMER BEFORE HE LISTENS TO YOU

If you are selling a technical product, you *must* know whether the buyer is as technical as you are. That will control the language (or jargon if you like) that you are able to use to get your message across. If the product has many applications, and most have, you must know which particular application your prospect is likely to be concerned with.

Always remember that rarely does anyone actually want the particular product or service that you are offering. What the average prospect does want is a solution to some kind of problem, and probably a very specific problem. Before you offer the answer, you must spend some time in discovering the question. At an exhibition you have limited time to persuade the customer that it is worth his while to stay with you and talk, and a 'Can I help you?' approach, which passes the initiative back to the buyer, will convince him he could be better off elsewhere.

As with all selling, but more importantly at exhibitions since you have less time available, the questions that you ask must always concentrate on the customer rather than the product. They must be aimed at securing, in an extremely short time, the information that for a normal selling application you would have acquired long before you made a face to face call. The initiative for your buyer to say 'no' and walk away must never be encouraged until you have decided that he is not a buyer.

TAKE ADVANTAGE OF THE DIFFERENT ENVIRONMENT YOU ARE IN

Exhibitions are a very special kind of selling but because the visit from the prospect is unsponsored and on his own impulse, they must in many ways be regarded as a better environment in which the seller can make his point. However, the initial contact does demand a different reaction and skill from the seller to ensure that full advantage is taken of the rarity of a buyer's approach to you. It is unfortunate that at most exhibitions, that skill is often not exercised.

CHECKLIST

- Demonstrations are not always the right answer.

- What is your prospect aiming to secure from a demonstration?

- Make sure the equipment you are displaying is faultless.

- Be aware of the different environment and demands of an exhibition.

- An early knowledge of your customer and his needs is essential.

14

The professional presentation

'*The great pleasure in life is doing what people say you cannot do.*'

Walter Bagehot (1826-1877)

It is a certain fact that if you, your presentation, or your customer approach is more professional than the competition, you will have a better chance of selling a product or service which may well be more expensive or even inferior to that of your competitors. You can build a successful operation with a poor product and enthusiastic and professional salespeople but there is no way you will succeed with a first class product and second rate salesmen. It doesn't really matter that the qualities on which your customer is judging you are irrelevant to the actual deal you are proposing. He is looking for professionalism as well as good value and he will judge that professionalism as much by the way you present your offer as by what you include in it. In the selling of a service, this is probably more important than almost anywhere else, as you have little tangible hardware to show. You cannot demonstrate as you can with a piece of machinery, and you cannot take your customer out to see the product in a different location. What you *can* do is to use the hardware that you have to your best advantage.

There is no doubt that the salesman promoting any kind of service has always envied his counterpart who sells say, stationery, and has something specific to show his customers. For a substantial part of my career with a large national company, I handled both a capital equipment division and also a service division and I am well aware how the service side suffered by not being able to display its wares. The financial investment markets in particular have a similar problem in offering something which is basically indefinite, the only real hardware being the written proposal at the end of the discussion. Between the initial introduction to the client and the production of that hardware, the salespeople in these professions have to rely solely on their own skill and personality in making that presentation.

MAKE USE OF WHATEVER HARDWARE YOU HAVE AVAILABLE

Whatever method you use, always be aware of the advantages of showing rather than talking. Your prospect will always look at a display with more attention than he will listen to your words. You will, of course, only be able to use such aids if they are readily available and it is vital that you consciously have them to hand so that you can use them in a professional manner.

I can recall many years ago the occasion when I purchased my first electronic calculator. This was in the earliest days of such equipment and indeed, until the salesman actually produced the calculator in my office, I had not even seen one before. I was then (probably more than now) quite capable of mentally handling the relatively simple calculations which my job demanded and certainly did not need any electronic assistance to make it easier. I was, however, intrigued by the persuasive approach of the representative who came to my office. He sold me the idea of buying a pocket calculator for £120.00 (a not insignificant amount in 1971), not to enable me to add up more accurately, but so that I could impress my customers with my professionalism. Indeed that calculator did just that. I was dealing with managing directors who, like myself, had never seen one before and who called in others to see it also. For the next few months at least, that hardware that I was carrying raised my reputation far more than anything I could have said.

The same psychology is still true today but in a different way, and it needs to be applied to all the equipment which we use in the presentation to our customers. Compare it, if you will, to directing a motorist on how to reach a certain town, and then carrying out the same operation with the aid of a map. Good as you might have been at the first directions, you will be immeasurably better at the second, and the motorist will have far better odds of reaching his destination.

Brochures are, of course, a visual aid in themselves, and taking a prospect through the brochure detail is something that few will need advice on. There are, beyond that, many additional aids which can be tailored to your own demands. For all applications, display books will hold a range of information, both in press releases and photographs of your product, including your own collected examples of similar applications elsewhere. The same book can provide details and prices of the service you are offering, with examples of different prepared sample prices to suit varying likely needs.

If your company advertises, then copies of recent advertisements provide a talking point while testimonial letters can always be usefully used. All the information needs to be collected from whatever sources you have, retained in one place and regularly updated. The main point is that it should be personal to yourself, and outside the usual company literature. Believe me, it will take you automatically into the visual sell, an advantage in itself, and also remind you of the way in which you best present your company image and product.

The briefcase that you carry needs to be clean and businesslike, and the literature that you take from it should always be kept separately in a folder so that it emerges clean and flat. Whatever you make use of in your daily work, whether it is an A4 pad (essential) or a pencil, make sure it is clean and looks professional. If you have to apologise for a chewed biro or a scruffy sheet of paper, *you are doing it wrong*. Overlooking small defects like this will affect the image you are aiming to project, and anything which harms that image can only make your job harder.

In many sales presentations requiring calculations, we have opportunities to impress with office and lap-top computers which, used properly, are capable of enhancing our presentation and adding a professional image to ourselves and our service. But, as with any presentation, make sure that you do it with style and don't forget that your reputation is capable of going in both directions.

HARDWARE GUIDELINES

The programming and use of hardware is not complicated and in a book of this nature, considering the wide variety of such computers in use, there is little point in giving anything but general guidance. However I believe a few general notes on the use of the equipment you are using would not go amiss.

■   **Treat it with respect** First of all you should always treat the hardware you have, whether it is a product or a means of explaining your service, *with respect*. This means handling it in a way which indicates that your company (or you) are prepared to invest in the highest quality equipment in order to sell to your customers. Treat your equipment casually and your customer will certainly notice and believe that the information it produces will be of the same standard.

- **Make sure you are competent** If you *are* using a lap-top computer in your presentation, don't fiddle with the controls as if you've never seen them before. If you really do not know how the equipment works, remember that the only reason that you have it is to impress your customer, and experimenting with it at his expense is likely to do just the opposite. Until you can use it effectively, leave it alone. After all, if you can't do the calculations in your head anyway, you probably shouldn't be in the job in the first place.

- **The information is more important than the equipment** If you are using a computer, don't make the mistake of introducing it on the basis of 'Look how clever this machine is'. If the client is impressed, he may well tell you so, but he is there to see the results it produces and a demonstration of the equipment itself will only sidetrack him from that objective.

- **Rehearse your presentation** Always remember that a sales presentation is no different from an act on the stage. If it is not to appear amateurish, it needs to well rehearsed in order to give you time to deal more competently with unexpected situations and problems for which you have not planned. Once you know what to expect from the equipment that you are using, your own confidence will help you cope with the unexpected that will always occur.

Remember that presentation and professionalism can often make up for deficiencies in the product or service you are offering, but if the presentation itself appears shoddy, then it will inevitably make whatever you are offering appear shoddy also.

CHECKLIST

■ Be judged as an expert; this means in the equipment you use as well as the knowledge you are promoting.

■ Look with empathy at your image and see yourself as others will see you.

■ Rehearse your act so that the equipment you use presents no surprises. Make sure that all the bits are there and that it *works*.

15

Getting your act together

'*No-one ever got far by working a 40-hour week. Most of the successful people I know are trying to manage a 40-hour day.*'

Channing Pollock

All you now need to do is to bring together all the advice you have been given in this book, add it to the experience you have acquired in the field and try to analyse why, in the past, you have failed when the business was placed elsewhere. It may well be that for whatever reasons, the loss of business was unavoidable and there is no doubt that in your career you will lose more business than you secure. Whatever the reasons, you can be sure that you will be more confident about the next deal if you have taken the trouble to evaluate the mistakes of the last one.

THE VALUE OF SELF CONFIDENCE

In many ways we underestimate the strength that confidence gives us, or the disastrous effect that the lack of it has on our selling success. A disappointing series of meetings or sales presentations can soon destroy our convictions about our product and it is essential that we learn how to be objective about the market we are in. George Bernard Shaw once remarked that, 'When I was young I observed that nine out of every ten things that I did were failures. To remedy the situation, I did ten times more work.' There *is* a solution to erecting your own defensive barriers against failure and to creating your own formula for success. In a simple word you can call it confidence.

Those of us who have worked for large companies are well aware of the effects of a well handled sales conference in the group. We all emerge with optimistic views of our future sales, optimistic ambitions about our new products and easy acceptance of the target figures which we are assured will now be well within our grasp.

Then what happens? We go out into the field over the next three days, we have four appointment rebuffs in a row, two sales taken by the competition and one customer who should have been a cast-iron certainty for the new product is let down by our administration department and takes his new business elsewhere. In a very short time, a series of 'no's means that it is a bad product, it is wrongly priced, and anyway, I've been given the wrong territory. All these factors have the effect of destroying the glowing view we had of the market and we approach our next customer believing, not that he will buy, but imagining all the reasons why he will not. Nothing new has happened to our latest customer that we should see him differently, he does not even know about our competition yet we are already visualising him taking the same action as all the rest. In short, we have lost confidence in our own ability to sell the product and have been influenced by many factors which really should not influence us at all.

RECOGNISE THE CONFIDENCE BREAKERS

Some of the reasons why we lose confidence are unavoidable. As I said above, you will not win every deal you go for, but many of the real confidence breakers come from weaknesses in our own selling and these can both be identified and remedied.

How many of us can honestly say that we are prepared for every question that the customer is going to ask about our product? In most cases our selling is relatively specialised and the facts and figures about our service, our equipment or our stocks are rarely that difficult to absorb and remember. Yet, sales professionals offering products about which they do not even have a basic knowledge is not unusual and any survey asking buyers what annoys them most about salesmen would put a lack of even simple product knowledge at the head of the list.

Remarkably, it would seem that many salesmen look at the extent of their product knowledge as something which, at best, they can get away with and at worst a liability which, with luck, will not lose them too many sales. But even if the customer does not notice, and maybe he does not have the technical qualifications to do so, the salesman's confidence in his own ability will have been eroded, and having lost that sale, he will go into the next one with even less optimism than he had before.

YOU MUST RESEARCH AND KNOW YOUR CUSTOMER

The same in-built weakness will be just as evident if you have not researched your customer, do not know what demands he is likely to make on you, if you are not aware what competitive product he relies on at present, and indeed if you do not know whether what you have to offer will benefit him or not. I can almost hear you reply that those are all things which can be unearthed during the first interview and indeed some of them can, but couple that lack of background knowledge with a lack of product knowledge also and you are really making hard work of your selling operation.

ACQUIRE ALL-ROUND KNOWLEDGE ABOUT YOUR PRODUCT AND THE COMPETITION

The confident and effective salesman will have at his fingertips *all* the knowledge assets. He will know his own products or services and will know the detail in the same way as an actor knows his lines. He will be totally informed on his competitor's products, their strengths and weaknesses and how those qualities affect those customers who use them. He will know whether the service the customers receive from those competitive suppliers is acceptable or whether it has left an opening where he, as a salesman, can offer an improvement. And he will know everything that he can about the business that he and his customer are both in, because for sure that is the one common ground where, from the start, they should be able to talk knowledgeably and competently with each other. Confidence based on that sort of knowledge is not acquired easily but it will still be around after the setbacks which will destroy a less well informed salesman.

At the successful end of a presentation, the salesman who does it all correctly will not seem to have sold at all. Without realising that he has actually been under pressure and has been directed down the road, the customer will believe that he has made the decision himself. This is *real* selling. Always leave your customer pleased that he has made the right decision and believing that the decision to buy was his and his alone. If the customer comes away reeling from the impact of the salesman's efforts and feeling that he has been bludgeoned into an order he might later regret, he might do just that and cancel the order the next day. (I am well aware of the law of contracts but you would be hard pushed not to accept a genuine cancellation if that is what the customer really wants to do.)

YOU MUST BE PREPARED TO CHANGE YOUR APPROACH

You must always consider how you can change your sales presentation, how you can look for different markets, how you can adjust to the conditions around you, and how you can alter your style of selling. In any career, it is easy to get into a rut, but in selling, due to the fact that you are generally away from company influences and authority, it is probably easier than most. Change, or at least consider change, all the time, and you will avoid the risk of developing standards and techniques which might possibly not be the best of which you are capable. In the words of Gellett Burgess, 'If, in the last few years, you haven't discarded a major opinion or acquired a new one, check your pulse – you may be dead.'

WORK UNDER PRESSURE

Persistence will always bring better results than the assumption that if you work an average day with average knowledge and average enthusiasm, then you should do at least as well as the rest. It is vital that you create your own pressure (otherwise someone in authority will do it for you) and make your own day as demanding as you are able. Remember that the number of contacts you make in the field is directly related to the number of orders you can count at the end of the month.

Essentially it all comes down to organising your time so that you can give selling the priority that it deserves. In your own daily organisation, always sort out the urgent jobs from those which can wait. This does not mean sorting out the short jobs from the long ones, simply because the first take up less of your time and so can be done without reference to their importance. It means that if the solution to a problem is not of consequence, then put it aside and handle it, if at all, only when the more pressing matters have been dealt with.

It is not, if you work at it, difficult to discipline your day so that you *do* increase the amount of time you spend face to face with customers. The routine that we all get into is probably the greatest barrier to making such changes but the only way that you will really upstage your competitors is to work with ideas which just do not occur to the average salesman. There *are* customers who will see you at eight o'clock in the morning (honestly), and similarly there are many others who will see you late at night. I agree that you might be pushing your luck to rely on those times as being generally available but ignore them altogether and you will lose the opportunity of many potential appointments. You might just be surprised how high a percentage of your customers are prepared to be seen at times that others might consider unreasonable. The real plus points are firstly, that your approach will indicate your enthusiasm, and second, you will be discussing your business at a time when you are less likely to be interrupted by others.

Selling *is* a skill like any other but unfortunately it has acquired the tag of being, like playing the piano, something you were born with. Believe that and you have been wasting your time reading this book. Realise that you can improve your knowledge and polish the skills that you have and you are half way to becoming the top salesman of tomorrow.

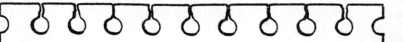

CHECKLIST

■ Build your own barriers against failure, but always know *why* you failed.

■ Knowledge and expertise build your own self-confidence.

■ Your selling must seem effortless, both to you and your customer.

■ Aim to increase your own face to face selling time. If you call more, you will sell more.